HOW TO

THE COMPLETE LIST OF THE

WRITE

40 CHARACTER ARCHETYPES OF COMEDY

FUNNY

AND HOW TO USE THEM TO CRAFT FUNNY

CHARACTERS

DIALOGUE AND CAPTIVATE AUDIENCES

How to Write Funny Characters

The Complete List of the 40 Character Archetypes of Comedy and How to Use Them to Craft Funny Dialogue and Captivate Audiences

ISBN: 9798714710445

For Gus

ALSO BY SCOTT DIKKERS

How to Write Funny

How to Write Funnier

How to Write Funiest

The Joke at the End of the World

*Outrageous Marketing: The Story of The Onion
and How To Build a Powerful Brand with No Marketing Budget*

Welcome to the Future Which Is Mine

Trump's America: Buy This Book and Mexico Will Pay for It

43: A Portrait of My Knucklehead Brother Jeb (by George W. Bush)
with Peter Hilleren

E-Day! The Funniest Screenplay Never Produced
with Jay Rath

Our Dumb World
with the staff of *The Onion*

Destined For Destiny: The Unauthorized Autobiography of George W. Bush
with Peter Hilleren

The Onion's Finest News Reporting, Volume One
with the staff of *The Onion*

Our Dumb Century: 100 Years of Headlines From America's Finest News Source
with the staff of *The Onion*

You Are Worthless: Depressing Nuggets of Wisdom Sure to Ruin Your Day

*The Pretty Good Jim's Journal Treasury: The (Even More) Definitive Collection of Every
Published Cartoon*

Plebes: The Cartoon Guide for College Guys

I Finally Graduated from High School: The Sixth Collection of Jim's Journal Cartoons

I Feel Like a Grown-Up Now: The Fifth Jim's Journal Collection

I Got Married If You Can Believe That: The Fourth Collection of Jim's Journal Cartoons

I Made Some Brownies and They Were Pretty Good: The Third Jim's Journal Collection

I Got a Job and It Wasn't That Bad: The Second Collection of Jim's Journal Cartoons

I Went to College and It Was Okay: A Collection of Jim's Journal Cartoons

Commix
with Kathryn Rathke, Chris Ware, J. Keen, James Sturm, Jay Rath

A HOW TO WRITE **FUNNY** BOOK

HOW TO

THE COMPLETE LIST OF THE

WRITE

40 CHARACTER ARCHETYPES OF COMEDY

FUNNY

AND HOW TO USE THEM TO CRAFT FUNNY

CHARACTERS

DIALOGUE AND CAPTIVATE AUDIENCES

SCOTT DIKKERS

TABLE OF CONTENTS

There is no me. I do not exist. There used to be a me but I had it surgically removed.

— PETER SELLERS

1

THE GREATEST ASSET IN COMEDY

We're all characters. We all have clearly identifiable traits that make us unique among our friends and family. Whether we like it or not, these traits often amuse the people in our lives. And we all know people in real life that we find amusing. "Oh, you know that crazy Uncle Jay—that's just the way he is!" we say. Characters in real life like Uncle Jay—and maybe like us—are vibrant, colorful, and hilarious. They're larger than life.

But have you ever tried to capture that lightning in a bottle and conjure up a character for a short story, a comic strip, or a script? It's not so easy. Somehow a lot of the magic of characters in real life is lost in translation. Our created characters fall flat, or don't ring true, or just aren't funny. They don't jump out at you the same way people in real life do, and they don't dazzle audiences like it seems our favorite characters from popular comedy movies or TV shows do so easily. When you try to write a funny character, it often feels uninteresting, and your audience doesn't connect with it.

Sometimes characters you write for a story don't work simply because they only serve the functions of your plot outline. They end up being cogs in your story machine with no uniquely relatable or amusing personality traits, and they don't act any differently from the other characters in your material. Or worse, they all act and talk like you, the writer, without any distinct voice of their own. Other times they seem to work well, but they lack originality, and come off as hokey or clichéd, no different from characters we've seen hundreds of times before in bottom-of-the-barrel comedies like kids shows or bad TV sitcoms.

If you want to write characters that pop off the page or screen and delight audiences, eliciting gales of laughter, this is the book for you.

After I wrote *How to Write Funny*, which is a broad introduction to the basic tools of comedy writing and how to use them to write volumes of bankably hilarious material, several readers asked me to elaborate on one small part of that book, the section on Character.

Character is one of the eleven "Funny Filters" outlined in *How to Write Funny*. The Funny Filters, which I define as the eleven different ways that an ordinary idea can be transformed into a funny idea, are the core to understanding humor writing. The simple formula for humor or comedy of any kind is to think of Subtext (that is, an astute opinion about something that's wrong with the world that you can express in a simple sentence) and then run that Subtext through one or more of these eleven Funny Filters. This seemingly simple process is what makes all humor work.

The Funny Filters, as well as the guidelines for how to use them, are explained in great detail in *How to Write Funny*, so that territory won't be retrod here. This book, however, expands on the Character Funny Filter and spells out in much greater detail how to create hilarious and memorable characters that come sparkling to life, command an audience's attention, and (most importantly) get laughs. Some of the other Funny Filters will be referenced here, since they can be used to enhance Character, so a working knowledge of all eleven Funny Filters is a helpful prerequisite for this book.

Among the Funny Filters, Character is the most powerful and the most popular. Humor and satire writers since time immemorial have used funny characters to illustrate their satirical points of view or elucidate their story themes. With Character, they do it through a made-up person the audience can relate to. This brings their writing to life in a special way. Audiences are so delighted by made-up characters, they're too busy laughing to notice the delivery of the writer's Subtext. Nor do they observe the inner-mechanics of a story. This is exactly as it should be, of course. Your audience should never see the gears inside your work. And they should never get your message straight, or "on the nose." That's bad writing. They should be shown, not told. Using characters is one of the most effective ways to show an audience what you have to say as opposed to telling them. Audiences simply want to enjoy the funny world you've created. They want, essentially, a funny puppet show. They don't want to be preached to by some comedy writer.

In the pages ahead, you'll learn how to use Character to manipulate the masses into laughing hysterically. You'll learn to move them emotionally. And you'll learn to communicate your ideas to them in a way that's purely entertaining. You'll learn how to master one of the most important tools of comedy.

If you've created a character and are looking to add traits and qualities to that character in the hopes of improving it, or if you're writing a funny story and need to create a new character to occupy it, this book will take you through a virtual turn-key process to create personality traits and quirks to appeal to the audience you're trying to reach. You'll learn how to hook audiences emotionally with your characters and get them personally involved. You'll learn to puppeteer this character to make audiences laugh until they can't breathe (but nonetheless survive).

In this book, you'll get actionable steps and a clear process for creating funny characters for any type of writing. You'll get examples from all media to illustrate how Character can be used most effectively, but the medium of movies is used most often. The logic behind this choice is (1) most of us are familiar with popular movies and they're easy to reference online, (2) making movies requires investments of millions of dollars, which means the producers and writers of movies are under enormous pressure to earn that money back. They can't afford to take chances experimenting with comedy that might not work. They have to use techniques so reliable that they all-but guarantee audiences will love their characters. This makes movies the best medium to study when learning how to create fun and engaging characters for any medium, be it prose, visual, TV, audio, the stage, or street art.

Crafting funny characters is a skill that anyone can learn. With the best practices laid out in this book, you'll be able to create as many different characters as you can imagine, and you'll be able to delight your audience endlessly.

FUNNY-CHARACTER TIP #1: DON'T MAKE JUST ONE
Creating funny characters is a skill like anything else. The more you do it, the better you get at it. Don't create just one character and expect it to be a masterstroke. It might happen, but you'll have better luck if you create several characters. Quantity is the key to quality in comedy. The more characters you create, the better your chances of creating a great one.

It's safe to say, after roughly 6,000 years of written comedy, 10,000 years of human civilization, and 2 million years of human culture, that all the conceivable character types have probably already been written. The jury is in. We know which kinds of characters delight audiences and which kinds bore them. The types of characters that bore audiences have been weeded out over the eons, so we don't see them in any of the great writing amassed over the centuries. The types of characters that delight audiences have survived and thrived, so we see them everywhere. There are certain Character Archetypes audiences find the funniest, and if comedy were a science and not an art, comedy writers would all know these Character Archetypes like scientists know the periodic table of elements.

Comedy is more of a science than people realize. And the best comedy writers do in fact instinctively know these Character Archetypes. The core of this book shares that knowledge, with definitions of the 40 funniest characters. They comprise the "funny character table of elements." These are the characters we see time and time again in comedy. They're audience-tested favorites. They keep coming back because they work. And you can rest assured they'll continue to work for the foreseeable future. Audiences love them. They've always loved them. And they always will love them.

But simply selecting a character from the list in this book—duplicating an established or well-worn Character Archetype—isn't going to meet the standard of any kind of professional comedy writing. Characters need to be unique. They need to be strikingly original. You can't afford to waste your audience's time with a character they've seen before. And just about any Character Archetype taken off a list of popular Archetypes is doomed to be a stereotype audiences have already seen hundreds of times. Such a character isn't going to dazzle anyone.

So how do the writers of today create fresh, seemingly original characters that tap into these successful Archetypes when all the best characters have already been written over and over again since the beginning of time? In chapter 5, you'll find 10 easy-to-use techniques for making beloved Character Archetypes sparkle with originality.

You'll start with the basic building blocks of the established Archetypes, and then you'll construct an original character using these techniques and others outlined in the pages ahead. You'll infuse it with characteristics that will give your audience a sense that they've never seen this character before, yet it will seem as familiar as their Uncle Jay. People will not only laugh at your characters, they'll remember them, and possibly even fall in love with them.

One thing you won't need to do when creating funny characters is write any elaborate character studies—pages and pages about what your character eats for breakfast, where they went to high school, or what happened between their parents that messed them up so badly. You're welcome to do that for dramatic characters, but comedy characters don't need any of that added labor. Comedy characters are simpler. The difference between comedic and dramatic characters is detailed in chapter 9.

In short, the craft of writing funny characters is easy. Let's get into it.

2

WHERE ARE THESE PEOPLE?

How do you come up with funny characters? This chapter lays out three simple methods step-by-step.

The first two methods come into play when you create a stand-alone funny character, independent of any existing work like a story or show that character is meant to populate. This is when you're just free-associating and you come up with an idea for a funny character that you might want to work into a story, or you just want to invent a character for fun. In either case, you can put this kind of character on a shortlist of ideas and figure out where or how to use it later. It becomes just another idea in your idea bank.

The third method is when you have an existing body of work and you need a character to fit into it. You may be looking for a funny character to appear briefly in a short story, or you may need a protagonist to star in a multi-episode TV series. The process for creating the character in either scenario is the same. It's the same method for any medium or format, from comic strip to advertisement, from street performance to major motion picture.

THE LIGHTNING METHOD

The first method is what I call the Lightning Method. You use this method when, without even trying, a funny character pops into your head. You may not even know the source or inspiration for this idea, and that's okay. This happens sometimes, but you can't always control it, so it's not a reliable way to regularly produce funny characters.

You can cultivate this occurrence of Lightning by doing free-associative writing exercises like the Morning Pages (which I detail in *How to Write Funny*), or by making a regular practice of writing 10 funny ideas every day. These kinds of habits stoke your creativity and train your brain to be more fertile ground for such inspiration. When that ground is laid, sometimes an idea will just hit you like a bolt of lightning when you least expect it—while driving, while showering, while anywhere.

When the idea hits you, write it down immediately before you forget it. Keep it safe somewhere. After a time, like a week or more, take a look at this character idea again with fresh eyes and see if it still amuses you. If it does, you probably have something worth saving. Cross-check the character with the list of Character Archetypes in chapter 4. Make sure it fits one or more of the Archetype definitions. If it does, you could have a potential lead character, a brand icon, or a property you can license down the road.

Proceed to chapter 5 to make sure your character is unique and not just a retread of a character we've seen before. This will likely involve tweaking something about the character. If the character doesn't fit any Archetype but still amuses you, you can still use such a character, but it's appeal is probably going to be limited. Save it in your back pocket when you need a bit player in a larger work, or a non-critical character in a smaller work like a short article or a single gag. That's probably all it's good for, which is fine.

Do you remember Wimpy from the Popeye cartoon? He's just such a character. He's a bit player with one random trait who doesn't fit neatly into any Archetype. His trait: he loves hamburgers. That's all there is to Wimpy. Such bit players aren't required to engage audiences the way a major character does. They can afford to be offbeat or silly. This book will focus more on major characters.

THE INTUITING METHOD

The second method is what I call Intuiting. This is when you spend dedicated time to sit down and write something funny. Instead of being struck by lightning without trying, now you're trying. You're sitting in front of blank screen or blank piece of paper trying to come up with funny ideas. To come up with a funny character, think of characters in your life, people you've encountered, or imagine a character you'd like to encounter. You can take stock of the funny people at your job or in your personal life who strike you as amusing. Or imagine the rich life of a stranger you saw. If you come up with a character that strikes you as funny, cross-check it with the Archetype list in chapter 4. If it matches one or more Archetypes, proceed to chapter 5 and use one or more of the methods there to make the character unique. Let this character sit on your list for a while, and then come back and look at it later. If it's still amusing to you, put it on a shortlist and save it until you need a funny character.

FUNNY-CHARACTER TIP #2: AVOID CURRENT-EVENTS REFERENCES

Characters that are too closely tied to currently popular personalities have a short shelf life. In the age of the 24-hour news cycle, so many celebrities that may seem timeless now could well be forgotten sooner than you think. If you want your characters to last, stay away from direct references to current political figures, sports heroes, or movie stars.

THE CASTING METHOD

The third method is what I call Casting. You already have some material. You just need a character to live in it. Since you have some preexisting requirements for this character, this method starts by looking carefully at your work. Look at the theme. Look at the other characters (if any). Look at the setting. Look at the style of humor you've established or that you're hoping to establish. Look at every aspect of your creation. Then, craft a character that clashes with all of it. In comedy, you want a character that contrasts with either their environment, other characters, the style of humor, or themselves. The best policy is to contrast with as many elements as you can. You might even explore a meta form of contrast, where the character contrasts with the audience's expectations of the work, or contrasts with the medium you're using.

Contrast in comedy is best when it's not just a light clash but a major clash of opposites. Comic contrast that's based on extreme opposites creates Irony, which is one of the eleven Funny Filters, and which brings sustained laughs to a character. It gives you a clash so wildly opposite that it's funny: a slob and a neat freak have to live together (*The Odd Couple*); a hip tuna fish thinks his good taste will make him taste good (Charlie the Tuna); a little boy and a ferocious tiger go everywhere together (*Calvin and Hobbes*); a six-foot-three human who thinks he's an elf leaves Santa's storybook workshop and enters the harsh reality of New York City (*Elf*); an awkward klutz tries to woo the woman he loves but screws things up with outrageous Madcap physical humor at every turn (*There's Something About Mary*). Note how each of these characters clashes with extreme opposing force with just about everything around them.

Every character in every work of comedy is different, so while there's no one-size-fits-all approach to creating a funny character, finding this contrast is one thing you will almost always want. For comedy to exist in a story, you need some kind of conflict, tension, or discomfort that comes from these contrasting elements. A plain, wishy-washy or compromising character who gets along fine with everyone and is totally happy in their environment is not going to be funny. You need a character who's boldly contrasted with several aspects of your work like two opposing poles of a magnet. Without this maximum heightened contrast, your character will fall flat.

Beyond contrast, your character also needs to align with the themes you're exploring in your material so that they serve the function of bringing your thoughts to life. This is, after all, the whole point of writing. You have something to say, so you need to be clear about it. You want your character's lesson or goals to dovetail with your thematic message. If your theme is about telling the truth, using a lawyer who's forced by magic to always tell the truth (*Liar Liar*) makes sense. If your message is the power of redemption, using a petty criminal who marries a police officer who together decide to kidnap a baby (*Raising Arizona*) gives you a lot to work with. If your satirical message is the injustice of bureaucracy, setting your story within the bureaucratic and rule-obsessed armed forces with a protagonist who's a pacifist (*Catch 22*) is a winning idea.

Finding a character that aligns with your themes and yet at the same time contrasts with as many aspects of the material as possible may at first seem like contradictory aims. The key to successfully completing these two somewhat disparate things is to strike the right balance and keep things simple. You can't afford to confuse audiences by making your work too complicated. Confusion is the enemy of comedy. In order to avoid confusing audiences, make some aspects of your work align and other aspects contrast. This careful balancing act will give you the best results.

For example, if you want to set a story in outer space, and you create a character who's a hard-working astronaut who does a good job exploring space, learning about space, and sending interesting data back to Earth, that's too much alignment and not enough contrast. It's a wishy-washy character. The result would be a boring story.

Let's say you want to set a story in outer space and you think it would create good contrast if you made your main character a human infant with no space suit. And to generate even more contrast, you make mission control angry with the baby all the time. And maybe you throw in an evil space monster that's trying to hunt down and destroy the baby for good measure. A helpless baby constantly besieged by deadly forces is probably too much contrast and not enough alignment.

The right balance might be an astronaut character who, unlike a baby, is someone the audience expects to be associated with outer space. This gives you some alignment. But for contrast, you can make that astronaut lazy or incompetent. This would thwart the audience's expectations. We expect astronauts to be Roger Ramjets or characters from *The Right Stuff*, but a lazy or incompetent astronaut is the opposite of that, so it gives us Irony. This is what the creators of *Moonbase 8* did. Or you can make the character an alien, another type of character that makes sense in the outer-space environment, giving you some alignment, but put him at odds with either his home planet or with Earth authorities. This is what the creators of *Men in Black* did. These are characters who align nicely with some aspects of the work, yet have enough contrast with other aspects of the work to create tension and keep an audience interested.

After you strike the right balance between alignment and contrast, your next step is to fill out the personality traits of the character. This is where most of the hard work is done in creating a funny character, and it's the make-or-break job of the comedy writer. What traits will be best? Which ones will make the character jump off the page?

That's what the rest of this book is about.

3

WHAT MAKES CHARACTERS FUNNY?

A few key ingredients go into making a funny character. The Character Funny Filter, used properly, is the most basic. If creating a character is akin to baking a cake, the Character Funny Filter is your three cups of flour.

There are also, of course, some secondary ingredients, like funny traits, funny ways of speaking, and funny ways of acting. These are your eggs, your butter, and your baking soda.

There are also trimmings, superficial things like funny hats, color schemes, or quirks that can generate laughs. These things are akin to the frosting, decoration, and presentation of your cake.

There's another major essential ingredient to every funny character, but a lot of beginning comedy writers fail to use it. This is your sugar. Even if you have all the other ingredients, without this sweetener, you'll have something that looks like a cake and seems like a cake at first, but it won't taste like a cake. It'll be a big disappointment.

First, let's measure out the flour. The way the Character Funny Filter works is simple: you establish a character's traits, and then you show the character acting on those traits. Every time your character acts according to their known traits, a laugh results. It's that simple.

Comedy characters are two-dimensional. They're not meant to be realistic or believable people. They're meant to merely represent a human failing, or an aspiration, or a behavior. They represent some aspect of the human condition. An audience doesn't need to get to know a comedy character like they would a real person. All they need to do is identify the character's two-dimensional traits in a single moment. If those traits were chosen with some contrast, some alignment with the story, and inline with a good Archetype, the audience will find it funny. A comedy character only needs about two to three basic traits in order for the audience to identify the character and start laughing.

Homer Simpson, for example, is dumb and lazy. Those are his two primary character traits. When the *Simpsons* writers show him napping during an important meeting, the audience finds that funny because he's behaving in accordance with his traits. When he's napping on the job as a nuclear power plant safety inspector, that's even funnier because the contrast, and therefore the tension, is heightened. The writers make a satirical point about the dangers of modern technology in the hands of dumb, lazy Americans.

For another example of how the Character Funny Filter works, imagine an improv scene. The performers ask the audience for a suggestion, and the audience calls out the word "happy hour." One of the performers now assumes a drunk character sitting at a bar. Another performer sits at the bar next to the drunk character, and the two actors improvise a conversation. The laughs will likely come from the drunk character. The character will be established when the performer teeters, hiccups, acts slow-witted, acts hazy, displays inordinate emotions like affection, or exhibits any other typical drunken behaviors. While extremely basic and even expected, these little demonstrations of Character will get some chuckles from the audience. The Character Funny Filter has been engaged: a character has been established and it is now acting in accordance with its key trait: it is drunk. There are tricks to making this character far funnier in the chapters that follow, but this is the no-frills foundation for how the Character Funny Filter makes people laugh.

> FUNNY-CHARACTER TIP #3: USE CONTRAST TO MAKE CONFLICT
>
> *We've all heard the sage advice that we need to put conflict in stories. It's true that conflict can keep audiences riveted, and it's essential in most stories. But how do you create conflict in a light-hearted comedy? Through contrast. If characters are the polar opposite of their environment, other characters, or just about anything else in your story, that contrast will create tension, and the tension will create conflict.*

There are a lot trimmings and superficial things you can do with a character that will make it funnier and elicit immediate laughter from an audience without much additional effort. Among them:

- Put a funny hat on them
- Put funny pants on them, either too baggy, too tight, or fashionably questionable
- Make them walk funny
- Give them a funny voice
- Give them a unique vocabulary
- Give them a goofy accent
- Make them an unusual size, weight, or shape.
- Give them a funny hairstyle
- Give them a funny go-to facial expression
- Give them a unique way they react to the things around them.

> • Give them any kind of superficial quirky
>   trait you want

These traits will get some laughs in the short term, but only for the first few seconds of an audience's exposure to the character. These trimmings can work as a hook, and might also be a convenient way for audiences to remember the character. But if you want a character to endear itself to your audience, to demand to be heard from again, to become a character people love, love to hate, or at the very least care about for the duration of your work, you need to add the key ingredient, the sugar. If you want to create a character that's not only uproariously funny but also seems to take on a life of its own, you need to take a big scoop out of the bag of Reference, one of the other eleven Funny Filters.

Among the Funny Filters, Character is the most commonly used. The vast majority of the jokes on TV sitcoms and movies use the Character Funny Filter. In the majority of unsophisticated comedy, the Character Funny Filter may comprise as much as 90 percent of all the comedic material. The Character Funny Filter is pervasive because it's not only simple to use, it's audiences' favorite. Of all the things in this world, the one thing almost all people are most interested in, by far, is other people. We love people, we love to watch people, we love to listen to people, and we love to laugh at people. We love people so much, the characters we fall in love with don't even have to be people at all as long as they're people-ish, like anthropomorphized animals, aliens, or inanimate objects. It doesn't matter. If they act like people, we're in.

In the drunken improv example, the character was extremely basic, but audiences will laugh at such a character nonetheless. They laugh because the character is familiar to them. They see either themselves or others in it. It's that familiarity that's tickling their funny bone. They feel bonded to the writer (or in this case the writer-performer) because they now realize they and the writer-performer have a shared experience. We've all been around drunk people, or we've been drunk ourselves. It's relatable. The same goes for all the Archetypes.

A simple character like a drunk can bring big laughs because it's an Archetype. Granted, the improv performers may not have worked very hard to make the character strikingly original (which you'll see how to do in chapter 5), but the character provides such powerful comedy shorthand that audience laugh anyway. When employed by skillful professionals, this same Archetype can be career changing. The Drunk Archetype was used to great effect in the hit movie *Arthur*, which got its star, Dudley Moore, an Oscar nomination for playing this Archetype.

Relatability is what the Reference Funny Filter is all about, and it's the magic ingredient—the sweetener—when creating compelling, funny characters.

The Reference Funny Filter is employed when the writer finds a commonality with the audience, an experience or observation the writer can refer to that the audience understands because they've experienced it or observed it themselves. Often it's just a small relatable moment like, for example, how satisfying it is to pierce a butter knife into a new jar of Skippy peanut butter to take the first serving out of it. Often it's much larger, like an observation about human nature or society, like wondering why or how our political leaders gained their power when they're not especially smart or competent people.

There are 4 different grades of Reference.

A grade-A reference is any mention of a small, relatable thing in life that points out a flaw in society or humanity, one that the audience hasn't heard before in quite the same way. It can be a reference to an idea about the way things are, or the way things ought to be, like, for example, the idea that even the most calm and civilized people turn into violent monsters when they're behind the wheel of a car. George Carlin has used this Reference a lot: "There's a lot of shit you have to put up with when you're driving. Like joggers. I've killed three of those motherfuckers myself." This Carlin line gets big laughs using a grade-A Reference (along with a dash of the Shock Funny Filter).

A grade-B reference is employed when a writer refers to things that don't offer any deeper commentary about human foibles, yet audiences still recognize them and can relate to them. An example of this kind of Reference is a current event, a new hit movie that everybody's talking about, an upcoming holiday, or the day's weather. A joke scarcely has to be made when using a grade-B Reference. Sometimes the audience will laugh as soon as they hear the current event referenced. They often don't even wait for a joke. Watch any late-night TV talk-show monologue and you'll see this phenomenon in action.

A Grade C Reference is a callback, which is employed when the writer or performer refers to one of their own jokes told earlier. This happens at the end of almost every 5-minute stand-up set. The comedian refers to a joke they told earlier in the same act. This almost always guarantees a hardy laugh for a closing line. It works because the comedian has referenced something only they and their audience have shared. It's a heightened form of Reference that is especially bonding.

A Grade-D Reference is the in-joke or local joke, which is a joke based on referring to an experience or observation that only the joke-teller and the audience have experienced, therefore no one outside of that exclusive and tiny group will get the Reference.

Referencing things in life that are funny and pointing them out to an audience is an extremely broad and effective way for a comedy writer or performer to find humor. The source material is literally everywhere. We all share so many of the same experiences in life. The standard and now clichéd way to start a stand-up bit is "Did you ever notice . . . ?" Whether they use this phrase spoken or unspoken, this is how a comedian opens the door to the Reference Funny Filter. They complete the sentence by pointing out a clever Reference, either grade A, B, C or D. And the audience laughs when they recognize the thing being referenced.

A good Character Archetype is closely related to the Reference Funny Filter in that the Character is themselves a Reference. They're someone people recognize. Sometimes it's a quality the audience recognizes in themselves, sometimes it's a quality they recognize in others. But it's a clear Reference either way. The audience doesn't realize consciously that they're recognizing the Character, but they recognize it nonetheless.

Comedy audiences love impressions. They love to hear a performer imitate a celebrity or politician, in voice, appearance, or both. Impressions are another type of Reference humor. Recreating the sound of a famous person's voice enough that audiences recognize it almost always gets laughs, even if the words spoken aren't particularly well-crafted jokes. It's the audience's recognition of the shared Reference that makes the impression funny. Well-crafted jokes on top of the impression is what separates the more successful impressionists from all the others.

You can make up zany characters who don't have any relation to any type of person who's ever existed, and you might succeed if that character is a bit player in your story. But such a character in a major role will probably fail to elicit laughs from audiences because you will have failed to engage the Reference Funny Filter. With random, unrecognizable funny traits, you might garner some short-term laughs. But if you can tap into a known Character Archetype, a character with certain traits that all people can identify with, you're well on your way to creating a funny character that audiences will not only greet with big, sustained laughs, they'll be willing to invest in that character for however long your story lasts.

The most successful funny characters fall neatly within 40 established Archetypes. These Archetypes embody the key characteristics that have been time-tested by audiences throughout the eons, and they're virtually guaranteed to win over audiences, if you use them right.

4

THE 40 COMEDY CHARACTER ARCHETYPES

As you'll see, each of these Archetypes has its own strengths and weaknesses as well as its own ideal application. Some are currently out of favor, some are in. But they're always ready to be revitalized by a new iteration. All of them have a proven track record of success with audiences for countless generations.

The arts, culture, and comedy exist for a reason. We need them. They're not just frivolous diversions. They provide moral guidance and give our lives a sense of order and structure that we wouldn't otherwise have. Comedy characters provide an essential service. They're manifestations of different ways of living. They allow us to compare and contrast different types of behavior when they're shown at their extremes. Sometimes the Character Archetypes teach us to push ourselves. Other times they teach us to moderate ourselves. Either way, the power of these characters to show us the right way to live (more often, by counter-example, the wrong way), taps a nerve deep within us that makes us crave these characters.

COMEDY CHARACTER ARCHETYPE #1: THE EVERYPERSON

The Everyperson is a reflection of the audience. They are the "straight person" of comedy, the one who reacts to the comedy more than they make it. They react as normally as can be expected given whatever outlandish comedy context they're in. In this way, the Everyperson is defined more by who's around them than they are by themselves. They're placed in a work of comedy to provide contrast with the silly, crazy, or jokey person(s), situation, or environment. In so doing, they bond with the audience, and that's how they get laughs.

An Everyperson makes a great lead character because the audience can identify with them and see your comedy world through their eyes. This is how the Everyperson is most commonly used. They're often used in comedy worlds that are wildly different from our own, providing a mooring mast for the audience's entry into that world.

The Everyperson can also be a small character in a work of comedy, placed in the mix simply to comment with reason and rationality on the absurd situations. Bill Murray's uncredited role in *Tootsie* is an example.

The Everyperson is used a lot in TV sitcoms. A common sitcom format is the "center and eccentrics" format, in which one sensible Everyperson Archetype is surrounded by crazy characters. The Everyperson gets laughs simply by reacting sensibly to these crazy characters. The list of classic sitcoms that use this format spans the history of television, from *The Dick Van Dyke Show* in the 60s to *Welcome Back Kotter*, *Happy Days*, and *Taxi* in the 70s, all the way to the *King of Queens* and *Arrested Development* in the 2000s.

More examples of the Everyperson:

Jack Lemmon in *The Apartment*.

Ben Stiller in the *Meet the Parents* movies.

Kristen Wiig in *Bridesmaids*

Luke Wilson in *Idiocracy*

Arthur Dent in The *Hitchhiker's Guide to the Galaxy*

Malcolm in *Malcolm in the Middle*.

How to use the Everyperson:

Use the Everyperson like a stand-in for the audience, as if they've been transported into your story, looking in on the crazy comedy world you've created. Their go-to mode is, "This is the most ridiculous thing I've ever seen!" and they're always trying to do something reasonable and relatable to cope with all the madness around them. The Everyperson is best paired with zanier characters, situations, and settings for maximum contrast. Every time the Everyperson has a "normal" reaction to a crazy person or situation, a joke beat results.

COMEDY CHARACTER ARCHETYPE #2 THE GROWN-UP CHILD

The Grown-up Child is an adult who behaves like a child. They're an adult, but they nonetheless stamp their feet, cry at the slightest provocation, and otherwise behave like a child. In general, they behave with far more exaggerated, unfiltered emotion than situations warrant. They're also innocent, naive, and silly.

The Grown-up Child is an extremely common character in comedy. They represent the inner child in all of us. Audiences love this charter because we can all identify with children. They're cute and lovable (and sometimes annoying), of course, but more importantly, we all have child-like emotions suppressed within us. It's cathartic to see them acted out. We have a deep longing to go back to the easy days when we could just cry and throw a tantrum instead of navigating our complex world through responsible behavior and reasoned communication.

Seeing a funny character act out as if they're a child also makes us laugh in recognition of how inappropriate the behavior is. On the other hand, we also have a strong emotional reaction to childlike behavior that we value as adults: emotional honesty, vulnerability, and playfulness. Seeing the Grown-up Child display these virtues reminds us how to connect with our inner selves and other people. And it shows us how to live a more passionate and fulfilling life

All the humor of the Grown-up Child comes from them acting like a child in every situation.

Examples of the Grown-up Child:

Will Farrell in *Elf, Step Brothers,* and *Old School*

Lilly Tomlin's character Edith Ann

Tom Hanks' character in *Big*

Adam Sandler in *Billy Madison, The Waterboy,* and *Little Nicky*

E.T. (a hybrid with the Know-It-All Archetype)

How to use the Grown-up Child:

Create a character that expresses immature, childlike qualities—especially undesirable qualities we've all grown out of. This extremely flexible character works in almost any application. For comic contrast, the Grown-up child is often put in adult situations. But for a different kind of contrast, they can be put in a childlike context (like when Billy Madison went back to elementary school in Billy Madison). They are often paired with an Everyperson (a functioning adult) for additional contrast, or they can be paired with another Grown-up Child (as in *Step Brothers*).

COMEDY CHARACTER ARCHETYPE #3 THE TRICKSTER

The Trickster plays tricks on other characters and sometimes on the audience. The Trickster usually has magical abilities, even in otherwise non-magical stories. The Trickster always wins, is never in any real danger, and always has a trick to get out of a fix. Often their most effective trick is simply their charm, which is so powerful it can be considered a type of magic.

The Trickster doesn't have to obey the same rules of society or even of reality as everyone else in the story. They can bend almost any rule to get what they want. They often have some kind of secret knowledge that no one else in the story has, and this knowledge gives them an unshakable confidence in their actions.

In movies and TV, Tricksters often do camera takes or talk to the audience. Breaking the fourth wall is just one of the many rules they can break.

The Trickster is a character that harkens back to African mythology particularly, with characters like Eshu and Ananse. But they're present in a lot of other myths and folklore traditions all over the world. Gods and demons like Loki (in Norse mythology and the *Avengers* movies) are often Tricksters. Lucifer is another famous example.

The Trickster often manifests as a fox or a hare. Dr. Seuss knew this, and made his Fox in Sox a trickster. Bugs Bunny is one of the most famous tricksters of all. Note how he always ended up with the upper hand against Elmer Fudd (or anyone else), and often used magic to best his opponents. Stories about con artists often channel the Trickster Archetype with a slightly watered-down version (in that their magic tricks are confined to reality).

Tricksters are intensely popular because they make audiences feel like they're getting a valuable lesson about how to avoid being fooled, or led down the wrong path in life.

Other examples of the Trickster:
Puck in *A Midsummer Night's Dream*
Willy Wonka
The Road Runner
Roald Dahl's Matilda
The Cat in *the Cat in the Hat*
Ferris Bueller (a hybrid with the Traveling Angel)
Bill Murray in *Stripes* (a hybrid with the Loser and the Clown)
Eddie Murphy in *Beverly Hills Cop* (a hybrid with the Traveling Angel)
Captain Jack Sparrow (a hybrid with the Lovable Scoundrel)

How to use the Trickster:
Create a character that tricks or fools other people in your story. Allow them to bend any rule to always end up on top, and never put them in any real danger. Make sure they always have a trick up their sleeve to get out of any situation. The Trickster can be a lead character or a supporting char-

acter. The more clever the Trickster's tricks, and the more fun the trickster has playing them, the better.

COMEDY CHARACTER ARCHETYPE #4 THE TRAVELING ANGEL

The Traveling Angel is a character that is perfect, who doesn't learn, grow or change in a story, even when they're the lead character. Instead, they cause other characters to grow or change. They do this either with their heroic deeds, their example, or sometimes simply by their inspiration. They're usually the main characters in a story, especially in episodic stories.

Traveling Angels usually have magical powers. This makes them an excellent hybrid candidate with the Trickster. However, the Trickster is more magical. The Traveling Angel's magic usually has clear limitations within the rules of the story. The Trickster's magic has no limitations. They can break the fourth wall. The Traveling Angel can't.

For a Traveling Angel character to work in a story, they must help another character (usually the protagonist) grow or change through some kind of revelation. In *E.T. the Extra-Terrestrial*, E.T. helps Elliott grow up. In *Ferris Bueller's Day Off*, Ferris helps his friend Cameron lighten up.

The Traveling Angel sometimes takes on the characteristics of a second Archetype, the Fish out of Water, because they often enter a strange world that they don't fully understand in order to help a character in that world. But this is not always the case. The Traveling Angel's primary trait is that they're a superior, unflawed presence who moves through the story and helps someone else.

To make the Traveling Angel Archetype unique, some storytellers give them a slight flaw or imperfection, or a minor revelation that causes them to learn or grow by the end of the story, but these things must be extremely small, otherwise the character is not truly a Traveling Angel.

Audiences love the Traveling Angel because it's a fantasy fulfillment character. We all want someone to swoop in and save us and make our lives better.

The Traveling Angel can also be a Traveling Devil, like the Devil in *Bedazzled*, or the Devil in the *Book of Job*. This is a character that comes into people's lives and makes them worse, and then moves on, never changing or growing themselves.

Other examples of the Traveling Angel:
Marty McFly in *Back to the Future*
Eddie Murphy in *Beverly Hills Cop* (a hybrid with the Trickster)
George Burns in *Oh God!*
Amélie
Clarence in *It's a Wonderful Life*
Cain in *Kung Fu*

How to use the Traveling Angel:

Use the Traveling Angel if the main character in your story is perfect and does not learn, grow or change as a result of the story, as would a normal protagonist. Make sure your story focuses on them changing the life of another character instead.

COMEDY CHARACTER ARCHETYPE #5 THE BUMBLING AUTHORITY

The Bumbling Authority is a character that has some position of authority in society, usually a relatively low rank, and who fancies themselves powerful and influential. However, in reality they're a bumbling fool. This is an extremely popular Character Archetype. It embodies the principle of "Afflict the Comfortable," mocking those who would lord over us, bringing them down a peg or two.

The Bumbling Authority often has some kind of insignia that they're compelled to show everyone: a badge, or ID, or certificate of some kind that proves they have authority. They're weak, so without this insignia, their deepest fear might be realized: that they would be reduced to the level of a commoner. They cling to this insignia for their self-worth. However, they don't realize this insecurity. It's subliminal. They swagger and throw their weight around, not realizing how ridiculous and ineffectual they are.

Audiences love to see authority figures lampooned, which is the sole function of this character. The Bumbling Authority Archetype symbolizes the established power structures of society. They become a lightning rod for audiences' mistrust of established authority structures or rules. They provide a much-needed release valve for our frustrations about the official constraints of society. Paul Blart, Mall Cop, is a recent example of this Archetype. Mall cops, one of the lowest level authorities in society, are ripe for ridicule. When they swagger like a powerful authority figure but then fall flat on their face, audiences are endlessly delighted.

Other examples of the Bumbling Authority:

Principal Rooney in *Ferris Bueller's Day Off*

Lt. Frank Drebin in the *Naked Gun* movies and *Police Squad*

Ralph Kramden on *The Honeymooners*

Ace Ventura, Pet Detective

Daffy Duck (when he assays roles as sheriff, space commander, and other authorities)

Buzz Lightyear

Ron Burgundy in *Anchorman*

The Onion, with its strict AP-style news voice

Officer Barbrady on *South Park*

The Reno police on *Remo 911*

Chief Wiggum on *The Simpsons*

How to use the Bumbling Authority:

Give a character a position of low-level authority in society who takes their position very seriously, and then make them a buffoon.

COMEDY CHARACTER ARCHETYPE #6 THE NAIF

The Naif is naive and innocent. This is a popular Character Archetype closely related to the Fish out of Water. The two are often paired, but they don't have to be. The Naif is distinct in that they don't necessarily need to be in a new environment. They're naive wherever they are. They're also childlike, but distinct from the Grown-up Child in that they don't necessarily get laughs by acting like an emotional child. They get laughs from being ignorant of the way the world works, and unaware of the consequences of their behavior.

The humor of the Naif stems from their lack of understanding about the world around them, but they are not comically stupid like the Dummy. They are often wise on some level (for contrast). They're merely ignorant of basic things about the world that more experienced people know.

The Naif amuses audiences because we see ourselves in them. We've all felt wide-eyed and innocent at times, especially when we were young. We can empathize with the Naif. On the flip side, the Naif gives us a safe distance from our innocent days, allowing us to laugh at our former inexperienced selves.

Examples of the Naif:
Chris Farley in *Tommy Boy*
Tom Hanks in *Forrest Gump*
Naven Johnson in *The Jerk* (a hybrid with the Dummy)
Peter Sellers in *Being There*
Steve Carell in *The 40-Year-Old Virgin*
Ben Stiller in *There's Something About Mary (a hybrid with the Klutz)*
Marilyn Monroe in *The Seven Year Itch* and *Some Like It Hot*
Rose on *The Golden Girls*

How to use the Naif:
Create a character who's innocent and inexperienced in the ways of your comedy world.

COMEDY CHARACTER ARCHETYPE #7 THE FISH OUT OF WATER

The Fish out of water is more of a story trope than an actual character with traits, but it's such a powerful trope and used with success so frequently in comedy, it deserves to be included on this list. It's akin to the Naif, but has one major trait that makes it distinct.

Like the naif, the Fish out of Water doesn't know much of anything about their environment. But unlike the Naif, the Fish out of Water is always in a new environment, and often acts strangely as a result, or wreaks havoc because of their ignorance of the rules of their new environment. The Naif, on the other hand, is not necessarily in a new world, and often behaves more "normally" in displaying their innocence.

The Fish Out of Water appeals to the audience's desire to feel confident in their understanding of the generally accepted (yet not often spoken) rules of society. It's funny to us to see someone who doesn't know the most basic rules of the world or society. It makes us feel glad that we're not in that position, and this is the springboard for all the comedy potential in this character. The Fish Out of Water can work in a scenario in which the world is familiar to the audience (like the mermaid in *Splash*), but it can also work in a scenario in which the world is strange, and the audience relates to the Fish Out of Water character (like Arthur Dent in *The Hitchhiker's Guide to the Galaxy*).

The Fish Out of Water can also be a handy device for storytellers to integrate exposition. Almost every story using the standard Hollywood myth structure will feature the protagonist entering a new world in Act II, and so almost every protagonist is part Fish Our of Water initially. They need to be shown the rules of the new world, just like the audience.

Other examples of the Fish Out of Water:
The Brother from Another Planet
The Terminator (a hybrid with the Jerk and the Fighter)
E.T.
Marty McFly in the 1950s in *Back to the Future* (a hybrid with the Traveling Angel)
Jeff Daniels in the *Purple Rose of Cairo*
Jack Lemmon and Tony Curtis in *Some Like it Hot*
Simon Pegg in *Shaun of the Dead*

How to use the Fish Out of Water:
Put your character in a strange world they don't know much or anything about. The humor derives from their confusion, and the inappropriate choices they make trying to adapt.

COMEDY CHARACTER ARCHETYPE #8 THE DUMMY

The Dummy is simply someone who's dumb. Someone who is not very bright is a delight to audiences because this character makes us feel smarter. While it's cruel and unacceptable to laugh at people in real life who aren't as smart as you, even though you may want to, it's perfectly fine to laugh at a dumb character in a comedy story. That's the important societal function this character serves:. They're the repository of such unacceptable behavior. It's fun to point and laugh at someone who's dumb, and a relief to be able to do it to a fake character in the safe environment of entertainment.

A Dummy can be a protagonist, but they're usually a supporting character. Almost every sitcom with an ensemble cast has "the dumb one," like

Joey on *Friends*, Ted Knight on *The Mary Tyler Moore Show*, and Woody on *Cheers*.

Jokes spring from the Dummy anytime they act or say something dumb, and the dumber the better. In comedy, Dummies are usually enhanced with the help of the Hyperbole Funny Filter to be far dumber than anyone could be in real life.

Other examples of the Dummy:

Elmer Fudd

Winnie the Pooh

Homer Simpson (a hybrid with the Slob)

Jim Carrey and Jeff Daniels in *Dumb and Dumber*

Kevin Malone on *The Office*

Cruiser in *Stripes*

Kelly Bundy on *Married with Children*

Brittany on *Glee*

Gilligan on *Gilligan's Island*

How to use the Dummy:

The Dummy character is extremely easy to use. You just have to make the character extremely dumb, ideally much dumber than a real-life person could possibly be. Anytime the character says or does something impossibly dumb, you get a joke.

COMEDY CHARACTER ARCHETYPE #9 THE KNOW-IT-ALL

The Know-It-All is a character that's uncommonly smart, typically found in societal roles or mythological categories that lend one to be smart, like wizards, professors, and wise old owls. But for Irony, the role can be flipped on its head, making children or pets into Know-It-All Archetypes instead.

Know-It-Alls need only be noticeably smarter than the other characters in your story. The smartest person in a duo of not-very-smart characters can be the Know-It-All Archetype, like Hardy in Laurel and Hardy, George in *Of Mice and Men,* or Harry (Jeff Daniels) in *Dumb and Dumber.* The Ironic contrast is a big part of the humor in these pairings. You can also use Hyperbole to get big laughs from a Know-It-All who is super smart, who exceeds the level of smarts you could possibly see in the real world. Anyone in a comedy story with encyclopedic knowledge, impossibly accurate recall, or a fast mind is a Know-It-All.

A lot of stand-up comedians take on the Archetype of the Know-It-All by being the widened, experienced chronicler of modern times.

Audiences love this Archetype because it comforts us to be in the midst of an expert. It can also make us feel smarter themselves, because we have access to this comically smart person. On a deeper level, it connects with a desire most of us share, which is to be smarter.

The Know-It-All can also serve a handy function in a story of being a go-to source for much-needed exposition. They can always explain why or how something in your comedy world works.

One challenge of the Know-It-All, when relying on this Archetype to create a protagonist, is how to make the character empathetic and not pedantic annoying. As a minor character, a Know-It-All can afford to be a nuisance, but as a protagonist they can't. See Chapter 7 for techniques on how to make audiences care about any character.

Other examples of the Know-It-All:
Sherlock Holmes
Mr. Spock (a hybrid with the Robot)
Indiana Jones (a hybrid with the Fighter)
Hermione in *Harry Potter*
The Professor on *Gilligan's Island.*
Doc Brown in *Back to the Future*

How to use the Know-It-All:
Turn a character into a Know-It-All by making them the smartest one in the bunch, or the expert in a given field relevant to your story.

COMEDY CHARACTER ARCHETYPE #10 THE JERK

The Jerk is a character that's mean, and they know it. They hate everyone else, but that's fine with them because they figure everyone hates them too. Being mean is part of their identity. It's an art form to them, a kind of game. Jerks make good villains, of course, but they also make fun characters you love to hate, especially when their meanness doesn't cross the line into disturbing cruelty. In the hands of a skilled storyteller, a Jerk can be a protagonist. *Despicable Me* and *Megamind* are key examples. Bill Murray's character in *Scrooged* is a Jerk. The Grinch is one of the most famous Jerks of all.

Audiences love the Jerk because they love to see examples of how not to behave. They relish this character's brazen flaunting of all the rules and laws of society. It's something we wish we could do, on some level, and we are able to do it vicariously through the Jerk.

The Jerk can have a change of heart at the end of a story and learn to be kind to others, but this isn't always necessary.

Other examples of the Jerk:

Mr. Burns on *The Simpsons*

Dr. Cox on *Scrubs*

The Queen Bee Heather in *Heathers*

Lucy from *Peanuts*

Biff in *Back to the Future*

Dwight from *The Office*

How to use the Jerk:

Make a character who revels in their unkindness toward others. If the Jerk is to be your protagonist, be sure to give them some empathetic qualities so that the audience cares what happens to them (see chapter 7). The audience doesn't have to like the Jerk, they only have to be interested in them enough to want to know their fate.

COMEDY CHARACTER ARCHETYPE #11 THE HERO

We often call the protagonist of a story the "hero," but Heroes are not always protagonists, and protagonists are not always Heroes. In comedy, it's more accurate to refer to the Hero as one of the trusted Character Archetypes. A Hero is someone who saves other people, does good deeds, is strong, confident, and takes charge. The Hero is comfortable in that role. They're selfless, courageous, morally unambiguous do-gooders who want to help everyone, and believe they can.

In traditional myth structure, the Hero goes on a journey and returns with some kind of magical elixir to save his people. In modern stories, the Hero can save any person or group, and the elixir doesn't have to be magical. It can be anything—special knowledge, a deed, a trinket.

The Hero differs from the Traveling Angel in that they can grow and change themselves, and often do, and they don't usually move on to another adventure after the story, which the Traveling Angel always does. Heroes stay.

While the Hero is the default Archetype for any superhero, the Hero doesn't have to have super powers. They can be a cop, a fireman, or anything. And a superhero doesn't have to be a Hero. It's an opportunity for comedy when they're some other, unexpected Archetype.

The Hero is perhaps the most deeply satisfying of all the Archetypes. It's popular across all forms of storytelling, from comedy, to drama, to epic. Joseph Campbell's extensive work on the origins of the Hero myth is required reading for any storyteller, most notably *The Hero with a Thousand Faces*. He demonstrates that this Archetype has been used as a central character in religion in every culture in the world since the beginning of time.

Other examples of the Hero:
Tim Allen in *Galaxy Quest*
Sully in *Monsters, Inc.*
Mr. Incredible
Underdog, from the TV series of the same name
Don Quixote (a hybrid with the Bumbling Authority)
Leslie Knope in *Parks and Rec*

How to use the Hero:
If you need a character to drive your narrative or save the day, the Hero is the way to go. But because the Hero is such a common Archetype, it should always be presented with a new twist (see chapter 5).

COMEDY CHARACTER ARCHETYPE #12 THE ROYAL

The Royal is a rich, privileged character who expects to be treated like royalty. In a lot of stories, the royal is an actual prince or princess. In others, merely a rich person or a person who believes they're above everyone else and expects to be treated accordingly. Their status can be real or imagined. They are sometimes snobbish, bratty, and entitled, and other times regal, dignified, and natural leaders, but they're always driven by the trappings of their high station in life.

The Royal can be a likable lead character or a hated foil. They can also be an insignificant bit player. In any role, the Royal provides excellent contrast with Archetypes like the Trickster and the Slob, who can introduce conflict and Irony by being dismissive of anything regal or dignified. Audiences never tire of the "Snobs vs. Slobs" story.

Audiences love to see a symbol of wealth and privilege knocked down a peg. For millennia, regular people, who make up at least 99 percent of the world's population, have both depended on and despised royals. It satisfies something deep with us to mock these characters. In comedy, even empathetic Royals are frequently humiliated and belittled for comic effect. They almost always get thrown in the mud at some point in every story—not symbolic mud, but actual mud.

Other examples of the Royal:

Richie Rich

Waldo from *Our Gang* / *The Little Rascals*

The Princess Bride

Dan Aykroyd in *Trading Places*

Ted Knight in *Caddyshack* (a hybrid with the Jerk)

Julie Andrews has been typecast most of her career as the Royal.

How to use the Royal:

Use the Royal for any character who has generational wealth or who expects to be treated in a special way because of their money or high social standing, real or imagined. Every time they assert their status or the trappings of it, you create a joke beat.

COMEDY CHARACTER ARCHETYPE #13 THE LOSER

The Loser is a character who always has bad luck. As soon as you think they've defied the odds and had more bad luck than is statistically possible, they get more bad luck. No matter how hard they try to be positive and create good karma, the Loser always fails. Nothing good ever happens to the Loser. This character is often the "Lovable Loser" when they're the protagonist, because someone who's an unlovable loser will have a difficult time earning the audience's empathy, which is the essential job of the protagonist. But in a minor role, a character can be an unredeemable, and pitiful loser played for comic effect.

Audiences love the Loser because we've all had bad luck, and we've all felt down about it. It's a universally relatable state, and it comforts us to see it happening to someone else instead of us, especially someone who doesn't even bother putting a positive spin on it. They just accept their sad fate and lower their head in defeat. In this way, the Loser serves as a salve for our low self-esteem. Being able to laugh at a made-up person's bad fortune is one of the go-to feel-good ointments in the medicine chest of comedy. (See more on this phenomenon in Chapter 7.)

Rodney Dangerfield's comic persona was the Loser. He got no respect, and every one of his one-liners hinged on this character trait.

As the lead character in a feature film, a Loser's luck often flips at the end and they enjoy wildly good fortune. Steve Martin in *The Lonely Guy* is an example. Although he begins the story as a Loser who can't find a soul mate, by the end he finds love, happiness, and success, and is no longer a Loser. But another Loser Archetype in the same movie, played by Charles Grodin, is not the protagonist, so Neil Simon (who adapted a non-fiction book for the screenplay), revels in Grodin's permanent Loser status to generate the movie's biggest laughs.

Other examples of the Loser:

Charlie Brown

Pierrot

Jack Black in *School of Rock*

George in *Seinfeld* (a hybrid with the Neurotic)

Bill Murray in *Caddyshack*

Terri Garr in *Tootsie*

Wile E. Coyote (a hybrid with the Klutz)

How to use the Loser:

Make sure your character never catches a break, and bad things happen to them so absurdly often that it's funny.

COMEDY CHARACTER ARCHETYPE #14 THE ROBOT

The Robot is either a literal machine character or a straight non-machine character who displays no emotion. This is the proverbial "straight person" of comedy, who gets laughs reacting with a straight face to silly things just as often as they do silly things themselves, but both reactions are well within the range of this Archetype.

The Robot makes a great protagonist or supporting character, and provides excellent contrast with any of the more overtly emotional Archetypes, like the Royal, the Loser, the Damsel, and others.

Robot Archetypes who display emotion are usually some other kind of Archetype mixed with the Robot Archetype. Commander Data on *Star Trek: The Next Generation* was a Robot but he was a hybrid with the Know-It-All and the Naif, making for a unique and appealing character who was the source for a lot of the humor on the show.

Audiences find the Robot Character Archetype funny because they're used to a world in which most situations elicit an emotional response, yet as we grow up we're expected to be less emotional. The Robot Archetype shows this extreme. On the other end of that spectrum is the Grown-up Child, which is the opposite of the Robot character.

Other examples of the Robot:

Buster Keaton

The Blues Brothers

Jack Webb in *Dragnet*

The Witcher

Jim in *Jim's Journal*

Leslie Nielson was often typecast in his later comedy career as the Robot (usually a multiple hybrid with the Bumbling Authority and the Klutz)

How to use the Robot:

Create a character who reacts with no emotion to anything that happens around them. The audience will delight in how this character reacts to funny situations with a straight face.

COMEDY CHARACTER ARCHETYPE #15 THE KLUTZ

The Klutz is a clumsy character. Every time they fall, bump into things, bonk their head, or cause other people to have any other such accident or pratfall, a laugh results. This is a simple, one-dimensional Archetype, so it's usually paired with another Archetype to make for a richer character, especially in a protagonist.

Someone who's clumsy is appealing to audiences because we've all been clumsy at times, and seeing someone else be clumsy transfers our humiliation safely to them. The Klutz earns our empathy quickly with their relatable and unfortunate trait, and they create instant Madcap (another of the eleven Funny Filters), which audiences love.

The Klutz is often a hybrid with the Nerd because the Archetypes are so similar. The difference is that the Klutz messes things up by being physically clumsy. The Nerd is simply not cool.

The Klutz is one of the "lower" Archetypes, which provides excellent contrast when paired with a "higher" Archetype. Note how Martin Short's Klutz character was paired with the Hero (Dennis Quaid), in *Inner Space*. Another way to pair an Archetype for contrast is within the same character. Don Martin's Captain Klutz was a Hero-Klutz hybrid.

Other examples of the Klutz:

Fred MacMurray in *The Absent-Minded Professor*

George of the Jungle (a hybrid with the Primitive)

The Pink Panther (both Peter Sellers' and Steve Martin's versions (a hybrid with the Bumbling Authority and the Dummy)

Lt. Frank Drebin in *Naked Gun* and *Police Squad* (a hybrid with the Bumbling Authority)

Ben Stiller in *There's Something About Mary* (a hybrid with the Nerd)

Chevy Chase's comic persona was the Klutz

How to use the Klutz:

Give your character the unfortunate attribute of being clumsy and causing a lot of wacky physical mishaps.

COMEDY CHARACTER ARCHETYPE #16 THE NEUROTIC

The Neurotic is filled with angst. They're worried about everything, assume everything will go wrong, and see the worst in everything. They're often a hypochondriac as well, might have a little bit of obsessive-compulsive disorder, and always get bent out of shape over the little things. This "Nervous Nelly" is a good Archetype to contrast with serious and dire situations in comedy.

While similar to the Loser, the Neurotic's losses are not real. They're all in their mind. And whatever situation they're in, whether good or bad, they find something in it to worry about.

Audiences love this character because we relate to them. We all have worries, and this character speaks our worries for us. We also love characters who allow themselves to be vulnerable about their failings. The Neurotic also makes us feel better about our own neuroses. Their cartoonishly exaggerated neurosis gives us permission to laugh about it and ourselves.

Richard Lewis uses this Archetype for his stand-up persona. Woody Allen did as well, capitalized on his stand-up fame to launch his movie career. Even movies he wrote but didn't star in featured Neurotic lead characters: John Cusack in *Bullets Over Broadway*, Will Ferrell in *Melinda and Melinda,* and several others. Albert Brooks followed a similar trajectory with his movie career.

Other examples of the Neurotic:

Felix in *The Odd Couple*

C3PO

Monica on *Friends*

Fear in *Inside Out*

Chuckie Finster in *Rugrats*

George on *Seinfeld* (a hybrid with the Loser)

How to use the Neurotic:

Make the character nervous about everything. Every time they express an irrational fear, you get a joke beat.

COMEDY CHARACTER ARCHETYPE #17 THE NERD

The Nerd is dorky, unattractive, lacks social skills, dresses or acts out of fashion, and is interested in nerdy things. The Nerd taps into a time in our past (for many of us, high school), when we were ridiculed for being unpopular, or interested in unpopular things, or things arbitrarily chosen by our peers as undesirable.

The Nerd is closely related to the Klutz and the Loser, and the three are often used interchangeably, but the Nerd is not necessarily clumsy or misfortunate. The Nerd is simply "uncool."

The Nerd was largely out of fashion after the 80s, as traditional nerds like Steve Urkel, with tape on their glasses and a keen interest in computers, became an overused cliché in comedy. But the Archetype was immensely popular for a reason. Audiences love seeing characters who are marginalized and mocked for their unpopular interests or out-of-fashion appearance. We all feel different and marginalized on some level, and the

Nerd is our avatar, allowing us to laugh at this part of ourselves.

Patton Oswalt has successfully reinvented the Nerd for his comic persona. Whereas in the past, the Nerd was an object of ridicule, Oswalt embraces the label and has tweaked the "nerdy" interests to music and pop culture as opposed to computers. He also got rid of the ever-present Nerd glasses.

The Nerd is often paired with the Lothario, creating hilarious Irony.

Other examples of the Nerd:

Christopher Mintz-Plasse in *Superbad*

Anthony Michael Hall in *16 Candles* and *The Breakfast Club*

George McFly in *Back to the Future*

Alyson Hannigan in *American Pie*

Napoleon Dynamite

Kevin Gnapoor in *Mean Girls*

How to use the Nerd:

Give your character a keen interest in unpopular or obscure things, and make them unpopular and unfashionable themselves.

COMEDY CHARACTER ARCHETYPE #18 THE LOTHARIO

The Lothario is a character who's always looking for sex. That's their one characteristic. The character gets its name from the 18th century play *The Fair Penitent*, where a character named Lothario seduces a woman and then betrays her. But the archetype doesn't usually betray anyone. They're just always horny.

In recent history, Lothario characters have been exclusively men interested in women for sex. But in comedy, the Lothario is any character who's on the hunt for sex: male or female, non-binary, gay or straight.

Audiences like the Lothario because it allows us to live vicariously through someone whose confidence in their animal sexual nature take them over. People giving in to their animal instincts is generally funny (invoking the Shock and Madcap Funny Filters). For an even more base Archetype, who behaves like an animal in all ways, not just sexually, see the Animal.

The Lothario Archetype can be a minefield for the unenlightened writer. Traditionally, this character has been a womanizer whose unwanted advances are more sexual assault than comical randiness. Examples are *Looney Tunes'* Pepe Le Pew and *Beetle Bailey's* General Halftrack. Modern iterations of this Archetype must display sexuality that is nonthreatening. It should be strictly comical, playful, and consensual.

Examples of the Lothario:

Many of the Muppets in *The Happytime Murders*

Burt Reynolds in Blake Edward's *The Man Who Loved Women*

Austin Powers (and Fat Bastard)

Melissa McCarthy in *Bridesmaids* (a hybrid with the Slob)

The Onion's Smoove B

How to use the Lothario:

Create a character who's always trying to have sex. The awkwardness or discomfort they cause creates a joke beat.

COMEDY CHARACTER ARCHETYPE #19 THE WEIRDO

The weirdo is the person who is eccentric. They're strange on purpose, either because they don't care what other people think of them, or they want to get a rise out of other people. The Weirdo is different than the Nerd, who is maligned for their unpopularity, and from the Kook, who is certifiably crazy. The weirdo is weird by choice. The comedy in the weirdo comes from their specifically peculiar behavior, ideas, or way they live their life.

The weirdo connects with audiences because there's a part of all of us that dreams of defying society's conventions and living however we choose. We admire people who do it and go all the way with it.

Weirdo characters are often secondary characters in comedy. They're a little too quirky to be protagonists most of the time.

Wes Anderson and David Lynch often fall back on the Weirdo Archetype in their movies, as does Tim Burton. Nicholas cage often plays weirdos, especially earlier in his career, as did Crispin Glover and Johnny Depp. Neil Gaiman often writes Weirdo characters in his books.

Other examples of the Weirdo:

Kramer on *Seinfeld*

Allie Sheedy in *The Breakfast Club*

Aubrey Plaza's comic persona

Almost any character played by Carol Kane

How to use the Weirdo:

You can have fun with the Weirdo and come up with any kind of random quirks of dress, behavior, or ideas that you want. Ascribe them to the character and let their freak flag fly. Every time they act unusual, you get a joke.

COMEDY CHARACTER ARCHETYPE #20 THE ANTIHERO

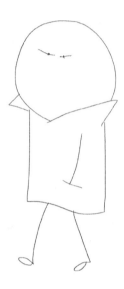

The Antihero is a protagonist who has charisma and leadership abilities, but doesn't use them, or uses them for selfish or immoral reasons. They could help people, but they don't, or can't, or won't. The Antihero might sometimes save they day, but they don't do it out of a sense of morality or to be the good guy. They do it either for the wrong reason, a selfish reason, or not at all. The Antihero is morally stunted, and any good deed they might do in your story is likely one of the only good things they've ever done in their life.

The Antihero is usually a protagonist. And they're usually on a mission like a regular Hero, and they're committed to their mission. They're also charismatic like a regular Hero. But their convictions are twisted, and their charisma is often used for nefarious purposes rather than good.

Antiheroes are fun characters we don't see enough of in comedy. This is partly because they're difficult to pull off, but mostly because they can come across too dark and disturbing.

Frank Miller likes making complex Antiheroes, like Batman in *The Dark Knight*, and most of the leads in *Sin City*. Hard-boiled detectives and noir characters are often Antiheroes. A lighter form of the Anti-hero is the Lovable Scoundrel.

Antiheroes don't often change or grow in a story, acting as Traveling Devils as opposed to Angels.

Other examples of the Antihero:

Sweeney Todd (a hybrid with the Jerk and the Sadsack)

Huckleberry Finn

Larry David on Curb Your Enthusiasm

Rupert Pupkin in The King of Comedy

The main characters on It's Always Sunny in Philadelphia

Malcolm McDowell in A Clockwork Orange

The main characters on The League

How to use the Antihero:

If you have a flawed or selfish Hero, go all the way and make them an Antihero, someone who solves the problems of your story for the wrong reasons, or for morally questionable reasons.

COMEDY CHARACTER ARCHETYPE #21 THE FIGHTER

The Fighter deals with problems by fighting with other characters, usually punching them in the face. This is another simple, one-dimensional character that works nicely as a bit player, but in order to be a more rounded protagonist, the Fighter needs to be a hybrid with another Archetype or two.

The Fighter appeals to audiences because we all sometimes wish we could solve problems with our fists, but the rules of polite society constrain us. We love living vicariously through characters who can get away with this kind of behavior, solving problems quickly and decisively with a little violence.

Any character who's a boxer, mob enforcer, or brawler is at least part Fighter. Most action heroes, super heroes, secret agents, and hard-boiled detectives are Fighters. Indiana Jones is a Fighter who's also a Know-It-All—another pairing of Archetypes that provides nice Ironic contrast.

(His only other trait is that he hates snakes.)

Other examples of the Fighter:

Clint Eastwood in *Every Which Way But Loose* and *Any Which Way You Can*

Robert Downey Jr.'s *Sherlock Holmes* (a hybrid with the Know-It-All, of course)

Number One on *The Umbrella Academy*

Mini-Me in the *Austin Powers* movies

Bob Barker in *Happy Gilmore*

How to use the Fighter:

Make a character who only knows how to solve problems with their fists. A common way to do make this Archetype fresh in comedy is to pair it with opposing traits, like kindliness, meekness, or small stature.

COMEDY CHARACTER ARCHETYPE #22 THE KOOK

The Kook is similar to the Weirdo and the Spacenut, but whereas the Weirdo is odd on purpose, or for effect, and the Spacenut is spacey, the Kook is downright insane. The things the kook says and does make no logical sense. They can be a hilarious source of Madcap non sequitur humor.

We all face societal pressure as adults to be sane, responsible, and buttoned up. The Kook is funny to us because we relish seeing someone breaking all those rules. We can laugh at their insanity, but we also admire someone who can say or do just about anything and still be comfortable in their own skin.

Examples of the Kook:

Steve Carell in *Anchorman*

Candidates for the Silly Party in Monty Python's "Election Night Special"

Tracey Morgan on *30 Rock*

Steve Martin in *The Jerk* (a hybrid with the Dummy and the Naif)

Jack Handy in *The Stench of Honolulu*

Lloyd Bridges in *Hot Shots*

Many of the characters in *Airplane!* were part Kook.

How to use the Kook:

Make your character spout non sequiturs and engage in behavior that makes absolutely no sense.

COMEDY CHARACTER ARCHETYPE #23 THE SADSACK

Not to be confused with the Loser, the Sadsack isn't necessarily unlucky in life, they're just sad. While the Loser is often optimistic, the Sadsack is a perennial pessimist, always ready to point out the worst-case scenario, or how everything will lead to their eventual despair or demise. However, the Sadsack is often paired with the Loser to make an extremely pathetic Sadsack-Loser hybrid.

The Sadsack is both clinically and comically depressed. You can always count on them to bring down the mood by expressing their negative feelings, which, in a comedy context, are funny.

Characters in fiction often serve a valuable mental health service, and the Sadsack is foremost among them. By depicting a comedic character who suffers from serious depression, mirroring the sad or depressed feelings we've all experienced, this character can make us laugh at our own depression, and in so doing, possibly uplift us.

Examples of the Sadsack

Eeyore

Marvin from *The Hitchhiker's Guide to the Galaxy*

Charlie Brown (a hybrid with the Loser)

Nicolas Cage as Charlie Kaufman in *Adaptation*

Oswald T. Pratt

How to use the Sadsack:

Make your character sad and depressed about everything. Every time they spin something to be sad, especially something that most people would consider positive, a joke results.

COMEDY CHARACTER ARCHETYPE #24 THE LOVABLE SCOUNDREL

The Lovable Scoundrel is charming, helpful, and always on the good side. But they flaunt their dismissal of the minor rules of society. They're often a petty criminal or otherwise operate outside of the strict letter of the law. They turn on the charm to achieve their ends, but they're blunt and impolite when they have nothing to gain. They're not afraid to "go low." Pirates and con artist characters often fit the Lovable Scoundrel Archetype.

The Lovable Scoundrel is lovable because they're doing what many of us wish we could do: follow only the rules we want to follow, and break the rest. We're attracted to naughty characters who can charm their way in and out of situations, and get away with cheating, especially when we sympathize with their motives. They have a smirk and a twinkle in their eye while they stick it to a corrupt society or established authority structure.

Examples of the Lovable Scoundrel:

Robinhood (a hybrid with the Hero)

Han Solo (note how he's paired with his comic opposites, the Royal (Princess Leia) and the Neurotic (C3P0), in the original *Star Wars* trilogy)

Captain Jack Sparrow (a Trickster hybrid)

Paul Newman in *The Sting*

Michael Cain in *Dirty Rotten Scoundrels*

How to use the Lovable Scoundrel:

Create a character who breaks a few laws and is generally a bad influence, but who ultimately falls on the right side of things and remains lovable throughout.

COMEDY CHARACTER ARCHETYPE #25 THE SLOB

The Slob is someone who's gross, messy, or doesn't take care of themselves. Any writer who tries to make a Slob Archetype empathetic enough to be a protagonist who can carry an audience through the entire span of a long story is in for tough road, but it's possible. Shrek is a successful slob protagonist. Characters in comedies or dramas will often "drop" into being a slob momentarily, while manifesting other Archetypes more prominently. (More on this concept in the chapter 6.)

Audiences find the Slob funny because it engages the Shock Funny Filter, tapping into the power of gross-out humor to get laughs. Also, we all on some level relish the idea of not having to take care of ourselves. It's relatable, and puts the character in a vulnerable position that we can't help but be attracted to.

Gross-out humor has a limited audience. Most people can only tolerate it in small doses. One way around this is to make a character a mild slob, so they can still exist in normal society and be lovable. This was done with Oscar in *The Odd Couple* and Seth Rogan in *Knocked Up.*

Other examples of the Slob:
Melissa McCarthy in *Bridesmaids* (a hybrid with the Lothario)
Pig-Pen from *Peanuts*
Bill Murray in *Caddyshack*
Zach Galifianakis in *The Hangover* movies
John Belushi in *Animal House* (a hybrid with the Animal)

How to use the Slob:
Give your character the trait of being messy, unkempt, or unhygienic.

COMEDY CHARACTER ARCHETYPE #26 THE PSYCHO

The Psycho is the violent or potentially violent crazy person, different from the harmless Kook by being an actual danger to others. And they're different from the Fighter in that their violence is disturbing and not in any way sportsmanlike or honorable. The Psycho usually only works as a protagonist in dark comedies. Jim Carrey in *The Cable Guy* is one example of this Archetype being stretched to the breaking point in a comedy, but in so doing the movie became more of a dark-comedy or horror-comedy. The Psycho Archetype abounds in horror stories that veer into the comedy space: Normal Bates *in Psycho*, Jack in *The Shining*, Dexter in *Dexter*.

Audiences have a morbid fascination with the Psycho. We can't take our eyes off them, because they live an amoral existence we find captivating from afar.

The Psycho is similar to the Jerk, but is identified more by their sick compulsion to do violence than their desire to be mean to people, which doesn't usually result in disturbing violence. The Psycho loves disturbing violence.

Audiences are drawn to the Psycho because it's a peek inside the dangerous part of all of us. Bill Burr plays the Psycho as part of his stand-up persona. In his more comic take on the Archetype, we know he would never do anything violent, but he has a lot of violent thoughts and fantasies, and a lot of anger.

Other examples of the Psycho:

Most of the family members on *The Munsters* (except Marilyn) and *The Adams Family*

Simon Bar Sinister on *Underdog*

The Terminator in *Terminator 2: Judgment Day*

Christopher Walken in *Annie Hall*

Francis (nicknamed "Psycho") in *Stripes*

How to use the Psycho:

The Psycho is a tricky Archetype to use while still remaining squarely in the comedy genre. If your Psycho character starts killing people or doing genuinely disturbing things, you veer into horror. To keep the character strictly a comedy Archetype, make their homicidal or sociopathic tendencies light, possibly never realized, and otherwise played for laughs as opposed to scares.

COMEDY CHARACTER ARCHETYPE #27 THE LEADER

The Leader is a common Archetype in both comedy and drama, and it's treated the same in both. The Leader is the alpha, the commander, the one who's natural charisma causes others to follow them and do what they say.

Audiences of both comedy and drama love the Leader Archetype because life can feel rudderless without them. We all crave the structure that the Leader provides. Although we often profess the opposite, on some deep level we all want someone to tell us what to do, where to go, and how to live our lives so we don't have to bear the responsibility. The Leader fills that role.

The Leader is the opposite of the Bumbling Authority. The Leader is a trusted authority, and their leadership is taken seriously, not mocked.

In comedy, anyone in charge is typically a Bumbling Authority, but occasionally you need a straight Leader, and that's where the Leader Character Archetype comes in handy. For example, on the classic sitcom *WKRP in Cincinnati*, Mr. Carlson, the owner, was the nominal boss of the radio station, and he was a Bumbling Authority. Andy Travis, the program director, was an actual Leader Archetype, played straight.

Dwayne Johnson often plays this Archetype, in both comedies and dramas. (*Baywatch, Rampage,* and *Journey 2: the Mysterious Island*)

Other examples of the Leader:
Gene Hackman in *The Poseidon Adventure*
Pappagallo in *The Road Warrior*
The King in *Coming to America*
Woody in *Toy Story*

How to use the Leader:
Give a character charisma, put them in charge, and make other people look up to them follow them or do what they say. This Archetype is best used as part of a comedy ensemble, and a good way to generate laughs with the Leader is to contrast them with painful weakness or insecurity.

COMEDY CHARACTER ARCHETYPE #28 THE PRIMITIVE

The primitive is someone who comes from a pre-industrial culture, usually a cave dweller. They don't understand modern social conventions or technology, and they often talk in the typecast way cave-dwellers talk, like saying, "Me want." It's this behavior that audiences find funny. Like many "lesser" Archetypes, the Primitive gives audiences a pleasant feeling of superiority when they subconsciously compare themselves to such an uncouth character.

The Primitive is not the same as the Slob. The Slob is merely messy. The Primitive may be messy, and have other Slob characteristics, but their primary trait is that they are primitive.

It's easy for this character to become a cliché. Entertainers have been wringing laughs out of the Primitive for generations without doing much to make it original. Phil Hartman updated this Archetype and made it fresh by ditching the Tarzan-like dialogue. Writer Jack Handy wrote the "Unfrozen Caveman Lawyer" as an articulate speaker, and this Irony made the character feel brand new.

Ben Stiller and Owen Wilson are "dropped" as Primitives in a scene in *Zoolander* when they're confounded by a first-generation iMac, hitting the computer and acting like chimps.

Other examples of the Primitive:

Tarzan the Ape Man

The Caveman characters in GEICO ads

The leads in the *Caveman* TV show

Brendan Fraser in *Encino Man* and *George of the Jungle* (the latter being a Klutz hybrid)

Tim Allen often descended into this Archetype on Home Improvement

How to use the Primitive:

Make a character act as though they come from a time before civilization. The laughs will come when they clash with the modern world.

COMEDY CHARACTER ARCHETYPE #29 THE SPACENUT

The Spacenut is similar to the Drunk in that they're often both under the influence. But whereas the Drunk is drunk on liquor, the Spacenut is either high on pot, acid, mushrooms, and other mind-altering substances. But not always, and not necessarily. Sometimes the Spacenut is just spacey.

The Spacenut is also similar to the Weirdo. The slight distinction is that the weirdo is quirky or unconventional, whereas the Spacenut is an airhead. Also, the Spacenut is naturally spacey; the Weirdo is weird by choice. The Spacenut is almost always made a hybrid with the Dummy, but this is not a requirement. Christopher Lloyd's Reverend Jim from the TV show *Taxi* was a smart Spacenut.

Audiences like this Archetype for the same reason they like the Drunk: it's funny to see someone who's not entirely present. It makes us feel good that we have our wits about us. On the flip side, it reminds us of when we or others were under the influence, which is something most of us can relate to and empathize with.

The lazy stoner Archetype has become an overused cliché in recent decades, so the Spacenut Archetype is out of favor at the moment. But all a writer has to do is a little original thinking, and suddenly this Archetype can feel fresh. Pixar's writers made the Spacenut feel original by forgoing pot as the reason for Dory's spaciness in *Finding Nemo*. They used short-term memory loss instead. This simple tweak breathed new life into this Archetype and made for a delightful and unique character.

Other examples of the Spacenut:

Jeff Spicoli in *Fast Times at Ridgemont High*

Cheech & Chong

The Dude in *The Big Lebowski* (a hybrid with the Loser)

Brad Pitt in *True Romance*

James Franco in *Pineapple Express*

How to use the Spacenut:

Make a character spacey but not dumb. The Dummy is someone with low intelligence, but the Spacenut is someone who's simply spacey or absent-minded. Any time they say or do something spacey or absent-minded, a joke beat results.

COMEDY CHARACTER ARCHETYPE #30 THE ANIMAL

The Animal is a character who acts like an animal, particularly an undomesticated one. They're often a Slob hybrid, but don't need to be. They have no manners, they shovel food into their mouths without utensils, and they might relieve themselves wherever they please. They generally make a mess everywhere they go. Whatever outrageous, uncultured thing they're doing, they don't realize they're violating any social norms. They're just acting naturally.

The animal is closely related to the Primitive, but it's slightly different. The Primitive has some rudimentary civilized aspects. The animal has none.

The appeal of this character is its pure abandonment of social norms and polite society. Manners and customs restrain us from our natural state as animals, so we love being reminded of what life was like in our primordial state. This character taps something deep inside of us that we long to reconnect with. By the same token, it reminds us just how inappropriate it is to behave like an animal, so it reinforces the idea that societal conventions and civilization are important things and we can be proud that we live up to them.

Examples of the Animal:

The Cookie Monster

Animal (from *The Muppet Show*)

John Belushi from *Animal House* (a hybrid with the Slob)

The Tasmanian Devil (from *Looney Tunes*)

Donnie from *The Wild Thornberrys*

Bert Kreischer taps into this Archetype for his stand-up persona

The Mermaid in *Splash*

How to use the Animal:

Create a character who takes on the qualities of a wild animal.

COMEDY CHARACTER ARCHETYPE #31 THE TOUGH

The Tough is the bad influence, the bad apple. They're someone who thumbs their nose at convention and goes their own way. They're usually charismatic, don't have to be. The Tough's singular function is to represent rebellious teen angst. They almost always wear a black leather jacket (a holdover from the 1950s, when Marlon Brando made this particular wardrobe choice stick in *The Wild One*). Dark sunglasses were added in the 70s and 80s when 50s nostalgia brought the character back into fashion.

The Tough is the younger brother of the Lovable Scoundrel. The key difference is that the Tough is on the bottom rung of society, with no real power. They're fundamentally weak, only pretending to be tough. The Tough is often brooding or hard-boiled like the Antihero, but the Antihero can exist in a comedy or a tragedy; the Tough is strictly for comedy, for three reasons: (1) the Tough is only two-dimensional, (2) the tough is never truly dark or unsympathetic, and (3) the Tough might be from "the wrong side of the tracks," but at the end of the day, it's all just a facade. They're actually just a softy.

This Archetype largely fell out of fashion after being overused in the 80s. But audiences will always have an appetite for the Tough. All it needs is a modern makeover, courtesy of one or more of the techniques in Chapter 5.

Examples of the Tough:
The Fonz
Andrew Dice Clay
Howard Stern's comic persona
James Franco in *Freaks and Geeks*
John Travolta in *Grease*

How to use the Tough:
Create a character who has a tough exterior, who goes against the grain of whatever social structure they're in, and who frequently gets in trouble for it. The laughs come from their lack of awareness that their tough facade masks a sad child on the inside.

COMEDY CHARACTER ARCHETYPE #32 THE DRUNK

The Drunk is closely related to the Slob, but the slob is not necessarily a Drunk, and the Drunk is not necessarily a Slob. Audiences find drunk people funny. Dudley Moore in the movie Arthur is a rare instance in which a drunk was used as a protagonist. Foster Brooks, a well-known comedian in the 60s and 70s, played a drunk in his stand—up. Any character can play the drunk when they're drunk, by momentarily "dropping" into this Archetype in a scene (see chapter 6).

The Drunk has fallen out of favor as a character since attitudes about drinking have changed, to say nothing of the serious problem of alcoholism and the horrors that come with it. But people still find this Archetype funny in short doses, because we can all relate to being drunk or being around drunks, and showing someone harmlessly drunk almost always gets a laugh.

Bridesmaids updated this Archetype and made it feel fresh by throwing in a sedative with the alcohol. *Toy Story* did the same by getting Buzz Lightyear drunk on imaginary tea instead of alcohol. *E.T.* mixed it up when Elliott got drunk by osmosis when E.T. got drunk.

Other examples of the Drunk:

Gary King in The World's End

Jonah Hill and Michael Cera in Superbad

The Onion's "Drunk of the Week"

Jada Pinkett Smith in Girls Trip

Dean Martin and Foster Brooks tapped this Archetype for their comedic personas

How to use the Drunk:

The Drunk is best used as a way to drop an otherwise sober, straight-laced character to create Ironic contrast. To make this somewhat out-of-date Character Archetype unique in any situation, get your character drunk via an unusual means, yet use the Reference Funny Filter by trotting out the tropes of drunk behavior that everyone recognizes.

COMEDY CHARACTER ARCHETYPE #33 THE CLOWN

The Clown is a character who always tries to make people laugh. This is their whole reason for being. The Clown Archetype is not the same as the comic relief character in a dramatic story. The comic relief character can be any kind of Archetype, including the Clown, which it often is. The Clown Archetype is different in that they live to bring laughter to others.

Actual clowns in street performances and in circuses are the Clown Archetype. Robin Williams' was a Clown in *Patch Adams*. Bill Murray is a Loser—Trickster-Clown in *Stripes*. Joaquin Phoenix's *Joker* character is an Antihero-Clown.

Every stand-up comic is some part Clown, since they're on stage to try to make us laugh. But the best comedians find another personality trait, often a complete Archetype, to differentiate their character from all the others, becoming a hybrid with the Clown and something else. For example, George Carlin was a Know-It-All–Clown.

The Clown has thrived since the beginning of entertainment since audiences love to be made to laugh. It cheers us up. But it's always in need of a refresh, since the traditional circus Clown with makeup was relegated to the hack bin generations ago.

Other examples of the Clown:
Billy Crystal in *Monsters, Inc.*
Robin Williams, not only in *Patch Adams* but in a lot of his movies
Jim Carrey in *The Mask* (and a lot of other movies)
Roberto Benigni in *Life is Beautiful*

How to use the Clown:
The Clown must always be focused on making people laugh. It can be a very one-dimensional character, so it's best to make it a hybrid with another Archetype to round it out if it's meant for a major role. As a pure Archetype, it works well in short pieces and pantomimes.

COMEDY CHARACTER ARCHETYPE #34 THE TOADY

The Toady is the fawning underling. They suck up to power, usually a specific person in power. Their identity is wrapped up in being a sycophantic servant beholden to another character.

Audiences love the Toady because they're a pitiful and weak Archetype that we can all relate to. We've all encountered people who have self-esteem so low that the only way they can feel good about themselves is to latch onto so someone superior and pump them up. While sad or even menacing in real life, we find this behavior funny in a fictional character.

The Toady can be the Henchman to any other Archetype, but most often they serve a Jerk, an Anti-hero, or a Tough. One way to make the Toady original is to make them a henchman to an entirely unexpected Character Archetype. As long as they fill the role of the Toady, this character will make audiences laugh.

Examples of the Toady:

Smithers on *The Simpsons*

Dwight on *The Office*

Detective Santiago on *Brooklyn Nine-Nine*

Dr. Steadman on *Scrubs*

The Minions

How to use the Toady:

Make a character kiss up to another character consistently, so that they're sole trait is that they serve, defend, or otherwise elevate the other character.

COMEDY CHARACTER ARCHETYPE #35 THE DAMSEL

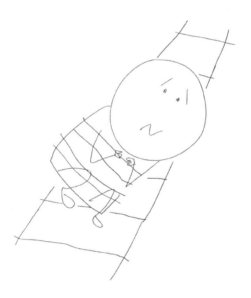

The Damsel is a character who's helpless and needs to be saved by a stronger character. We've obviously seen the cliché in old movies where the Damsel was always a distressed woman tied to the railroad tracks by the mustachioed villain in a black cape. But that doesn't mean this Archetype is dead or no longer relevant. In the 70s, master storyteller Mario Puzo updated the character by making her tough and independent, with Lois Lane in his story for the first *Superman* movie. The makers of *Journey 2: the Mysterious Island* updated the Archetype further by making it a man (Luis Guzmán in a hybrid role of Damsel-Toady). These little tweaks made this tired Archetype seem original.

Audiences like the Damsel because it fits so well with one of their favorites, the Hero. It provides a critical role in the fantasy fulfillment for both characters, regardless of which side of the rescue fantasy you prefer.

It's a simple, one-dimensional character that's always worked.

Examples of the Damsel:

Polly Purebred from *Underdog*

Olive Oil from *Popeye*

The Princess Bride

Shaggy and Scooby from *Scooby Doo*

How to use the Damsel:

Put them in trouble, helpless to save themselves. The audience will expect the Hero of your story to save them. But be careful to update this Archetype, because the weak and helpless woman Damsel is a cliché.

COMEDY CHARACTER ARCHETYPE #36 THE BUREAUCRAT

The Bureaucrat is someone who blindly follows the rules of society or the workplace, or any other construct, no matter how small, and no matter the outcome. In comedy, the outcome of blind rule following is usually hilarious, outrageous, or disastrous. The Bureaucrat is closely related to the Bumbling Authority, but with one key difference: the bureaucrat is in charge of nothing. They're so low level in a bureaucracy that they often have no one working underneath them.

Like the Bumbling Authority, the Bureaucrat taps into our deep mistrust of governing bodies and rules. We all have instincts to obey rules yet also disobey rules. This conflict within us is never fully settled, no matter where we fall on Kohlberg's scale of moral development. Some of us are still obeying rules because we fear punishment. Others among us only obey rules if we feel they're worthy of being obeyed. Whatever the case, it's fun for us to see someone slavishly obeying all rules, no matter the significance and no matter the outcome. It guides us to find peace with our own relationship with society's rules.

Examples of the Bureaucrat:

The Sloth from *Zootopia*

Steven Spielberg in *The Blues Brothers*

The bus driver in *Quick Change.*

Yubaba in *Spirited Away*

Many of the Characters (other than the protagonist) in *Brazil*

How to use the Bureaucrat:

Make your character a stickler for every rule and regulation, no matter how small. Every time they stick to a rule that's a joke beat.

COMEDY CHARACTER ARCHETYPE #37 THE CRANK

The Crank is closely related to the Jerk, but whereas the Jerk is defined by their immoral behavior toward others, the Crank is simply in a bad mood.

Quick to anger, quick to insult, and never willing to forgive or give lee-way, the Crank shows us a side of ourselves we all share, but that most of us have learned to control in polite society. When we went through our "terrible twos," we had tantrums and screamed and cried like a Crank so we can relate to this Archetype much like we can to the Grown-up Child. What makes the Crank distinct from the Grown-up Child is that the Crank doesn't engage in any other childlike behavior. They're just a Crank.

Seeing a comedy character brazenly behave the same way is satisfying on two levels: (1) we wish we could still get away with it, and (2) it makes us feel good about our choice to grow out of our cranky instincts and be a polite member of society.

Examples of the Crank:

Archie Bunker

Oscar the Grouch

Donald Trump

Anger in *Inside Out*

Lou Grant (and a lot of comedy bosses)

How to use the Crank:

Create a character who's rude, grouchy, and always finds things to complain about.

COMEDY CHARACTER ARCHETYPE #38 THE COOL CAT

The Cool Cat is someone who is extremely cool, or at least thinks they are. They're smooth, confident, and slick.

The appeal of this Archetype is that we all wish we were cooler. We're all embarrassed about being awkward, so to see someone who never has an awkward moment is inspiring. It shows us how to breeze through life without a worry.

The Cool Cat is often so cool that they can persuade anyone to do just about anything, and they often have magical powers. Sometimes they even break the fourth wall by being so cool, like Ferris Bueller does. This makes the Cool Cat a natural hybrid with the Traveling Angel.

The Cool Cat often has their own slang that includes made-up words or rhymes so hard to understand that it's like a different language, which can confuses other characters for comic effect.

To create Irony, the Cool Cat is often contrasted with the Neurotic, the

Nerd, or the Loser, either by pairing two characters or by "dropping" the Cool Cat momentarily into one of these lesser Archetypes.

Examples of the Cool Cat:

Pootie Tang

The Ant in *The Ant and the Aardvark* cartoon

Steve Martin and Dan Aykroyd's "wild and crazy guys" from SNL

Reginald Perrin's son Mark on *The Fall and Rise of Reginald Perrin*

Jean Ralphio Saperstein on *Parks and Rec*

Mike Damone from *Fast Times at Ridgemont High*

Larry on *Three's Company* (a hybrid with the Lothario)

How to use the Cool Cat:

Create a character who keep their cool and remains relaxed in all situations to a comical degree.

COMEDY CHARACTER ARCHETYPE #39 THE PARENT

The Parent is a simple Archetype used interchangeably between Moms and Dads in comedy. The parent is a dorky, overly caretaking embarrassment to their children. Although they try to be "with it," they're hopelessly uncool with their shows of genuine emotion and their bad jokes. The children of the Parent usually take on the Everyperson Archetype so the audience can identify with them, making the two-dimensional Parent(s) a laughing stock.

It's a good feeling and an important life transition to establish our independence from our parents, especially for teens and young adults, who are likely just emerging from some two decades of living under parental tyranny. This makes for fertile ground in comedy. We may have at one time thought of our parents as near god-like, and mocking them provides a much-needed release valve on the stress of growing up.

"Dad jokes" and the Parent in general have been overused in recent years as entertainers have discovered just how popular this Archetype is. One way to make it unique is to assign different Archetypes to characters who are parents. While Jerry's parents fit the Parent Archetype on *Seinfeld*, George's mom was a Kook-Parent hybrid, and his dad was just a Kook. Elaine's dad was a Psycho-Tough. All of these supporting-characters' parents had elements of the Drill Sergeant. Another way is to apply the Parent Archetype to a character who isn't a parent. Whether it's a boss, lover, friend, or enemy, the audience will recognize the tropes of the Parent Archetype and you'll get laughs by using the Analogy Funny Filter. In a lot of comedies, especially body-switching comedies, the kids take on the Parent Archetype while the parents become the Grown-up Child. This is such a successful formula we've seen this movie dozens of times

Other examples of the Parent:

Chevy Chase in *National Lampoon's Vacation*

Will Ferrell and Amy Poehler in *The House* (they proceed to transform into Toughs, a novel way to update this Archetype)

Jon Arbuckle in *Garfield*

Richard Belding in *Saved by the Bell*

How to use the Parent:

Make a character that deeply cares for another character while at the same time embarrassing them by acting like a doting parent.

COMEDY CHARACTER ARCHETYPE #40 THE DRILL SERGEANT

The Drill Sergeant is a character who orders people around with no mercy. While the Drill Sergeant is a mean person in charge, they are neither the Leader nor the Jerk. They're different from the Leader in that they don't necessarily have charismatic leadership qualities. They're different from the Jerk in that, in almost all cases, they have a heart of gold if it's ever uncovered. And if it is, it's only in secret, never in front of the entire group. The Drill Sergeant may scream and hurl insults, but in the end, they love their "recruits."

Audiences appreciate this character for the same reason recruits in the military respect their drill sergeants. It's oddly comforting to us to hear someone scream insults at us and force us to be disciplined. On one level, it makes us feel more secure to know we don't take the insults personally. In fact we find them funny and even somewhat motivating. We all like to be held to a high standard.

Examples of the Drill Sergeant:

Beulah Ball-breaker in *Porky's*

The alarm clock in *Groundhog Day*

Mr. Garvey in *Key & Peele*'s "Substitute Teacher" sketch

Sergeant Hulka in *Stripes*

Otis on *Martin* (a hybrid with the Bumbling Authority)

How to use the Drill Sergeant:

Make a character who screams orders at underlings unrelentingly. We often see this character as either an actual military drill sergeant or a tough inner-city schoolteacher. To avoid these clichés, apply this Archetype to a different kind of person or object, like Harold Ramis did in *Groundhog Day*.

As the writer of a funny character, you'll always connect with audiences if you use one of these Character Archetypes. But as with all comedy writing, you must follow a few basic guidelines. The most important of these is to avoid clichés. If you've seen one of these Archetypes too much, or if you think an Archetype is out of fashion, you can either avoid it and chose a different one, or you can bring it back in fashion with a twist. All you have to do is tweak the Archetype around the edges. No fundamental alterations will be necessary. You'll get easy techniques for how to do this in the next chapter.

5

10 ARCHETYPE MAKEOVER TECHNIQUES

The first step to creating a character that will delight audiences is to choose an established Archetype that's proven to be an audience favorite. The second step is to make that Archetype feel unique, which can be challenging given that these characters are well-worn and have been battle tested in every medium of entertainment for centuries. But as you'll see, it's surprisingly easy to make audiences perceive your Archetype as strikingly original.

These 10 techniques are small hinges, but they swing big doors. A little tweak to a character can make all the difference between a character who's a cliché and a character who breaks the mold and becomes a big hit. These 10 techniques are in no particular order.

1. Create a hybrid

By combining one or more Archetypes, you increase the likelihood that audiences have never seen that particular combination of traits before. Suddenly the 40 Archetypes give you hundreds of possible combinations.

When you combine Archetypes to create a hybrid, experiment with both Irony (opposing traits) or Hyperbole (exaggerated traits). The Ironic Nerd-Hero is a popular Archetype of recent years, in movies like *Nacho Libre* and *Superbad*. Andy in *The 40-Year-Old Virgin* is a Naif-Grown-up Child hybrid. Basil Fawlty is a Loser-Bumbling Authority Archetype. The hyperbolic Naif-Fish-out-of-Water hybrid has always been popular, from *Mr. Smith Goes to Washington* to *Borat*.

James Bond, one of the most enduring comedic characters of the last century, is another Archetype hybrid. Ian Fleming threw everything into the pot for James Bond, making him an almost irresistible mix of Trickster, Lothario, Fighter, and Know-It-All.

When you mix and match the Archetypes to create a hybrid, be sure all the traits of each Archetype are present in the character.

2. Make the Archetype a different race, ethnicity, species, or gender

This method may seem superficial, but it's extremely effective in making audiences think you've created an original character.

In recent years, a lot of successful new characters have been old comedy favorites re-introduced as women. Female Fighter-Hero hybrids, especially in sci-fi action stories, have been a mainstay now for decades, yet audiences still find them fresh. Melissa McCarthy's character in *Bridesmaids* was one of the first female Slob-Lothario hybrids audiences had ever seen.

Sheriff Bart in *Blazing Saddles* was an original character that shocked White America in the 70s: a Black Hero. Mel Brooks upended decades of Hollywood tradition with a Black Western sheriff to great comic effect. He milked the Irony, setting up the character's entrance to the town with an elaborate welcome ceremony in which all the White townsfolk gather, only to be shocked and horrified when they see that he's Black.

There are so many Archetypes that could do for a makeover by being gay or transgender. This is a trend that's already churning out beloved characters. Characters with tradition-busing gender or sexual orientation have been popping up in entertainment for years now. Billy Crystal played one of the first openly gay characters on TV in the 70s on *Soap*, as the

Everyperson. Marvel introduced a gay Hero in *The Eternals*. These characters not only serve audiences ravenous for cultural representation, they also get talked about in the media for their breaking of new barriers. But the skilled writer knows they're just different versions of the same characters audiences have loved for eons.

Mr. Peabody was just a regular Know-It-All, an already overused Archetype when he was introduced in the late 50s by Jay Ward, but he felt original because he was a dog. E.T. was the standard Fish Out of Water, but he felt new because he was an alien. Chewbacca, also an alien, gave new life to the Animal Archetype.

Think about a new race, gender, or species you can assign to your character to make it a groundbreaking original.

3. Make the Archetype a different age

Characters we normally associate with one age range can feel all new when we put them in an unexpected age group.

A teen superhero is suddenly a fresh take on a well-worn superhero Archetype, as seen in the *X-Men Origins* series. A middle-aged Archetype that we usually see young is almost always funny, as it was with the aging Mr. Incredible.

Audiences are grateful when they meet an Archetype in the form of an old person or a child. Macaulay Culkin as the Trickster in *Home Alone* was a huge hit with audiences. Bamm-Bamm, a child Primitive, was a popular character introduced in later seasons of *The Flintstones*. Alfalfa, of *The Little Rascals*, is a Naif-Lothario hybrid. Blanche on Golden Girls is also a Lothario. Comedic moments were created in Ron Howard's *Cocoon* by "dropping" the older characters into Lothario Archetypes for a scene or two.

Consider making your older character a Naif or a Dummy, or a younger character a Know-It-All, Weirdo, or Crank. These are unexpected pairings audiences will love.

4. Put the Archetype in a different genre

Certain Archetypes tend to adhere to the same storytelling genres. As trends come and go, writers over-use particular Archetype-genre pairings until audiences get tired of them, and then they fall out of fashion. Being conscious of these trends and riding them or bucking them can make your characters seem unique.

In comedy, genres are all hybrid genres or sub-genres, like action-comedy, romantic-comedy or sci-fi comedy. The Royal is often found in romantic comedies. George Lucas put one in a sci-fi adventure (Princess Leah in *Star Wars*). Charlie Kaufman put an Everyperson, an Archetype usually found in reality-based stories, into a mind-bending fantasy in *Being John Malkovich*. The creators of *Big*, Tom Hanks' breakout movie, put a Grown-Up child in a romantic comedy, which was the first time a lot of audiences had seen that. The creators of the *Jumanji* reboot made the Hero and the Royal and the Neurotic feel original by both putting them in the new genre of the RPG-action-comedy, but also by making them different races, genders, and ages than we normally see, mixing them up in the bodies of typecast characters that contrasted to create Irony: The Neurotic became the Royal in Jack Black, and the Nerd became the Leader-Hero in Dwayne Johnson.

Superman and Spiderman are well worn characters, but their built-in genre-defying Archetype hybrids have delighted comic book readers for decades, and continue to delight new movie audiences every time they're rebooted. They're both Heroes with nerdy secret identities, Irony that audiences almost never get tired of.

5. Give the Archetype a different job or position in society

This is another seemingly superficial change that can transform an Archetype into something fresh. Ace Ventura is a Bumbling Authority, but he's a pet detective, a job we've never seen before. Paul Blart is also a Bumbling Authority, but he feels unique because we'd never seen that Archetype as a mall cop before. Buddy is a Naif and Fish out of Water, which we've seen endlessly, but we'd never seen it as an elf. The Men in Black are Robots, which we've seen before in secret agents and policeman, like on *Dragnet*. But this particular job-Archetype pairing had fallen out of fashion. To bring it back with a facelift, the creators made the Men in Black not just police or secret agents, but *intergalactic* secret agents, which we'd never seen before. Homer Simpson's job as a nuclear safety inspector is not only an original job for a Dummy Archetype, it's dripping with satirical Irony.

The hilarious *Midnight Run*, starring Robert De Niro and Charles Grodin, paired two Archetypes in jobs we'd never seen before. De Niro is an Everyperson-Jerk hybrid, a unique mix with great inherent contrast, and he has a job we've never seen an Everyperson hold (though we may have seen a Jerk with it from time to time), that of a bounty hunter. Grodin plays a Neurotic who worked for the mob, another job–hybrid pairing with great inherent contrast.

You can also make a character unique simply by putting them in a different socioeconomic group. *Pygmalion*, *My Fair Lady*, and *Down and Out in Beverly Hills* all succeeded in creating captivating characters by turning a low-status Slob into a high-class Royal..

FUNNY-CHARACTER TIP #4: KEEP CHARACTERS SIMPLE

You may be tempted to mix a lot of Archetypes in order to create a truly great character. Don't overdo it. Audiences will get confused if you use more than three or four Archetypes in one character at the same time, especially if they don't mesh. You can "drop" them into different Archetypes (see chapter 6) but it's best to limit the ones you use for each character. Audiences are easily overwhelmed. They need to be spoon-fed. They're not paying as close attention to your work as you are. Keeping things simple and easily digestible for an audience is always the best policy.

---

6. Give them a new and different physical appearance or voice

A simple, superficial change to an Archetype like a look or sound is sometimes all it takes to give it a fresh face. Find a distinctive way for your character to talk or a certain physical appearance that's different from what we've seen before. Michael Palin in *A Fish Called Wanda* added a stutter to accentuate the Neurotic Archetype. The Swedish chef on *The Muppet Show* made the Klutz Archetype new with his nonsensical fake

Swedish speech. *The Princess Bride* is filled with standard Archetypes who all seem unique because they have a distinctly unusual bearing or speech, from Wallace Shawn's lisp to Mandy Patinkin's accent to André the Giant's size.

Rowan Atkinson is a master of this technique, creating original characters based off of well-worn Archetypes with a slight affectation in his voice. His largely pantomimed Mr. Bean made the Grown-up Child feel original by not speaking much at all, and his exaggerated upper-crust British accent in *Never Say Never Again* made his Naif-Bumbling Authority Archetype one of the funniest characters in any James Bond movie.

7. Give them a different way of manifesting their traits, or a different reason why they have their traits

The traits of an Archetype are what audiences crave, and these traits can be reintroduced in new characters endlessly without ever seeming hacky as long as the traits are manifested or justified in a unique way. This can be as simple as changing the medium in which the character is introduced, or using a different format where they're presented. Other times, it can be more involved, incorporating their backstory. To illustrate this method, I'll use two characters I created that became popular.

The first is Jim, the titular character of my comic strip, *Jim's Journal*, which appeared in hundreds of newspapers and lead to a *New York Times* best-selling book collection. It also inspired the creation of Jeff Kinney's *Diary of a Wimpy Kid*. Jim was a hybrid Robot-Everyperson Archetype, and was made original in two ways. First, He used a unique way of speaking, largely pantomime. But he also manifested his traits in a unique way. He expressed his views of the world and of the other characters in the comic strip through a first-person narration, a journal or diary format that had never been seen before in mainstream comics.

The second is the character of Smoove B, which I created for *The Onion*. Smoove B, the Lothario Archetype, quickly became the most popular of *The Onion*'s fake columnists. He was made original by communicating his traits through a newspaper column. This was a new medium for the

Lothario. His stilted writing and awkward descriptions were a player's attempt to convert seductive banter to the formal written word, where it lost a lot in translation and became funny.

Dory in *Finding Nemo* is another example. She's the Spacenut Archetype, but she had a memory problem instead of being high. The character felt fresh because she attained her primary trait in a new way.

Michael Scott (of *The Office*) has elements of the Klutz Archetype, but his Klutz traits are manifested not physically like the traditional Klutz, but through social awkwardness and a comical inability to read people.

Superheroes use this method a lot. So many superheroes have the same power (super strength, super speed, etc.), but they attain their traits through different means. This and a slightly different colored costume is all it takes to make their Archetypes seem distinct. Most of these characters are the constantly retreated Hero Archetype, but they're made original simply because they have different ways in which they attained their powers: the Hulk through gamma rays, Superman from the Earth's yellow sun, Spiderman from a spider bite, and so on.

8. Give them an additional trait on top of their standard Archetypal traits

Often, simply the addition of one small, specific trait unconnected to an Archetype's main traits will be enough to make that Archetype feel brand new to audiences. Ideally one of the 11 Funny Filters assists to make the trait hit the funny bone. Any Funny Filter is worth trying, but Irony is almost always effective. A Sadsack could be eternally optimistic about one particular thing, like Charlie Brown and the football that he always thinks Lucy will let him kick.

Superman could easily be a bland Hero Archetype, but a specific trait that contrasts with his primary trait (he's weakened by Kryptonite) has made him an endlessly interesting character for generations. James Bond, who should be focused on saving the world, always takes the time to make sure his martini is shaken, not stirred. This particular and unnecessary trait incorporates the Misplaced Focus Funny Filter. Both Doyle Redland, *The Onion*'s radio news man, and Ron Burgundy share the specific and hilarious trait that they will read anything that's put in front of them.

Indiana Jones is one of the most brilliant comedic characters to be con-cocted in the last few decades. He's a hybrid of the Fighter and the Know-It-All. His creators, masterminds George Lucas and Steven Spielberg, gave him one additional, random trait that isn't associated with any Archetype, and it gives him the flavor of a character that transcends Archetypes, mak-ing him feel like a one-of-a-kind creation. That trait: he hates snakes. It's a dose of both the Irony and Reference Funny Filters to give this worldly adventurer a silly and irrational fear. It's funny because it's the opposite of what you'd expect (the Irony Funny Filter), and it's relatable since so many of us also hate snakes (the Reference Funny Filter).

By mixing and matching traits with different Archetypes, you'll make unique characters: a Klutz who insists on wearing impossibly high-heeled clogs (Hyperbole and Madcap); a Know-it-all who doesn't understand the concept of humor (Metahumor); a Trickster who acts out scenes from their favorite stories (Parody). Find the combination that makes for the most humor or emotional engagement in your story.

9. Employ specific Funny Filters when your Archetype acts or speaks

There are countless ways to make characters unique by applying differ-ent Funny Filters to them. You can lean heavily on one Funny Filter for a character, making it their go-to way of speaking or acting. You can define your character and give them a signature style this way. Arnold Schwar-zenegger's Terminator, a great comedic character, is a Robot-Fighter hy-brid who uses the Reference and Irony Funny Filters almost exclusively for some big laughs throughout the *Terminator* franchise. Bill Murray and Eddie Murphy used Metahumor by breaking the fourth wall in their hey-day as big-screen Tricksters.

This method works particularly well in stand-up, in the forming of a unique on-stage persona. Anthony Jeselnik uses Misplaced Focus almost exclusively in his jokes. Weird Al uses Parody. Bo Burnham uses Metahu-mor as well as music. Not since Steve Martin in the 70s and 80s have we seen this combo. Audiences therefore perceive it as unique. Eric Andre and Any Kaufman are largely defined by their use of Antihumor.

10. Bring an Archetype back after a long absence

Sometimes a character can be made fresh merely by bringing it back after a long absence. If they haven't seen an Archetype in a long time, audiences forget how much they like it. Certain Archetypes fall out of fashion for one reason or another, and are always ready for a triumphant return.

The Lothario was popular in the 60s, with Pepe Le Pew, James Bond, and General Halftrack, among many others. But it fell out of favor as attitudes toward unwanted sexual advances evolved in the clear light of the women's movement in the late 20th century. The Archetype seemed hopelessly out of date and distasteful. But then Mike Meyers resuscitated it with great success in *Austin Powers* without having to use any more complicated techniques to make it feel original except to add a Metahumor element that allowed the audience to laugh *at* the anachronism instead of *with* it.

When *Star Wars* came out in the 70s, such tropes as the Royal in sci-fi, which had been used a lot in the 30s, had fallen out of fashion. Lucas reintroduced it with Princess Leia. He did the same with Han Solo and the Lovable Scoundrel Archetype, which had primarily been seen in swashbuckling stories up to that time, not space operas. He made both Archetypes feel new.

Melissa McCarthy's character in *Bridesmaids* seemed incredibly fresh because we hadn't seen a major Lothario character in pop culture since *Austin Powers* debuted some 15 years earlier. Her character also updated the Slob, which *Shrek* resurrected after a long period of being out of fashion when it debuted some 10 years earlier. Both Slobs and Lotharios are almost always men. So by making the character a woman as well, she utilized more than one technique to make a striking original and hilarious character.

Usually one generation, about 25 years, is plenty of time to wait before resurrecting an Archetype that's fallen out of fashion.

By simply employing one or more of these 10 techniques, your by-the-numbers Archetype will seem exciting and new. But making an Archetype feel new is only the first hurtle in creating a character audiences will laugh uproariously at. The next hurtle is making sure your character acts funny. In the next chapter, you'll see how that works.

6

CHOOSING AND USING THE ARCHETYPES

Funny characters based on one of the 40 Archetypes will generate plenty of laughs simply being who they are. Your audience will expect them to act in accordance with their traits. With the traits of each Archetype clearly spelled out, you now have a clear blueprint for writing your character. Show your Dummy act dumb, your Weirdo act weird, or your Royal act stuck up, and you're putting the Character Funny Filter into effect to make a funny and engaging character. Here are some examples of this process in action, with various Archetypes:

                    JOHN

    General Hansen?

                    STELLA
    No, I'm not a general, but may I help
    you?

                    JOHN
    Yes. I want to thank you for saving my
    life over in Vietnam.

```
                    STELLA
          I don't think that was me.

                    JOHN
          You're right. It was Normandy Beach. I
          was shot up pretty bad. You grabbed me,
          pulled me into a foxhole and patched me
          up.
```

That's Bill Murray's Trickster hybrid character in *Stripes*, trying to charm (that is, trick) an attractive young military police officer. He's also a Clown and a Loser, and both of those traits are in effect as well, the Clown trying to make her laugh, and the Loser covering up for his lack of actual military experience by lying about it.

Here's another example:

```
                    TRISHA
          I wanted to thank you for the beautiful
          drawing you did of me. It's hanging in my
          bedroom.

                    NAPOLEON
          Really? Took me, like, three hours to
          finish the shading on your upper lip.
          It's probably the best drawing I've ever
          done.

                    TRISHA
          Yeah, it's really... nice.
```

In just one line, Napoleon Dynamite clearly acts like a nerd. Humor results because he's the Nerd Archetype.

And another one:

```
                    MAX (V.O.)
          I'm the luckiest dog in New York, because
          of her. That's Katie. Katie and I . . .
          Well, we have a perfect relationship. We
          met a few years ago.

          Katie sees Max in a box marked "free puppies" on the
          sidewalk.

                    MAX (V.O.)
          And, boy, let me tell you, we got along
          right away. You know, it was one of those
          relationships where . . . Where you just
          know. And get this. She was looking for a
          roommate, and so was I! So, I just moved
          in that same day! Was perfect! We've been
          together ever since. Katie would do
          anything for me. And I'm her loyal
          protector.

          Max barks a pigeon on the sidewalk, only to get spooked
          by it and cowers by Katie.
```

                    MAX (V.O.)
          Our love is . . . Our love is . . . How
          do I put this? Our love is stronger than
          words. Or shoes.

Katie lifts up a chewed shoe and glowers at Max, who's in
the closet chewing all her shoes.

                    MAX (V.O.)
          It's me and Katie. Katie and me. Us
          against the world. I wouldn't go so far
          as to call us soulmates, even though, any
          sane person who saw us would.

MONTAGE

-- Max getting excited to see Katie

-- Max licking a dinner plate

-- Max moving his legs while dreaming in bed next to
Katie

-- Max licking her face as they look at the skyline
together.

                    MAX (V.O.)
          There's just one little problem. Pretty
          much everyday . . .

Max pulls on her to prevent her from leaving their
apartment.

                    KATIE
          Come on, Max!

                    MAX (V.O.)
          . . . she leaves!

                    KATIE
          I'll see you tonight.

                    MAX (V.O.)
          Sometime I try stuff to get her to stay.

                    KATIE
          Okay, sit.

Max sits.

                    KATIE
          Spin.

Max spins.

                    KATIE
          Speak.

Max barks.

                    KATIE
          Okay, that's a good boy.

                    MAX (V.O.)
          But, it never works! Where is she going?
          What could she possibly be doing? I miss
          her so much!

Max in *The Secret Life of Pets* is a Naif-Everyperson. He's inexperienced and doesn't understand the world, and here he is not understanding how the world works, making it extremely relatable to the audience by using the Reference Funny Filter, demonstrating so many of the recognizable tropes of being a dog.

FUNNY-CHARACTER TIP #5: TRAITS DON'T MAKE A CHARACTER, ACTIONS DO

You must show, not tell. What you show your character doing matters. They must always act in accordance with their Archetypal traits in order to establish which Archetype they are. But to continue to lure your audience further into your story, your characters must also act obsessively to pursue the outcome of their drive, the one thing they're after that propels your story. The planets will align when your protagonist's every action not only reinforces their traits but also drives the story forward.

As you can see, the dialogue in these scenes from popular comedy movies is not composed of gags. In fact, there's not a single gag here. The lines are simply the characters acting in accordance with their Archetypal traits. That's what makes them funny. These are Character jokes, and that's the magic of the Character Funny Filter. Jokes are not required as long as Archetypes are chosen well and act accordingly.

If you need a character to be a protagonist or a significant lead in a longer work (a movie, stage play, novel, or TV show), don't risk reinventing the wheel by thinking of an original character that doesn't match up with one of the 40 Archetypes. Chose an Archetype that fits your story. This is your fighting chance of making a connection with an audience, creating a character they'll feel comfortable with, be entertained by, and be willing to follow through a lengthy journey.

If you're working on a smaller funny character, like one that only appears in a single scene, short story, or short article, you can use an Archetype in that case too, but it's not necessary. You can afford to invent a new character from scratch. Just assign one to three random traits to a character and see what best enhances the humor of the work at hand. With smaller characters, you *can* reinvent the wheel, avoid the Archetypes, and be as offbeat and experimental as you want. But Archetypes should always be used when you need a major character in a longer work. The purpose of characters in that context is to bond with the audience, and Archetypes are the way to do it.

STORY FIRST OR CHARACTER FIRST?

You can write a story first and then populate it with characters, or you can come up with a character first and then build a story or comedy world around them. There's no right or wrong way to do it.

When it comes to brainstorming ideas for anything—stories, characters, or jokes—you're likely in the messiest part of the creative process, where dozens of ideas are being thrown at the wall to see what sticks. Tips and best practices for brainstorming are contained in the free ebooks available on <u>howtowritefunny.com</u>. To summarize here, the fewer restrictions or editorial judgment you impose on this first stage of the creative process, the better. To stimulate the most fruitful creativity, write whatever comes into your mind and see where the muse takes you. Later, after the dust settles, sift through all your ideas to pan for the good stuff. However you brainstorm ideas, always save any funny characters or funny stories you invent. You never know when you might come up with one that fits the other perfectly.

To find an Archetype that fits in your story, think in terms of contrast. Contrast creates Irony, and therefore laughs. If your story is grand and sweeping, a diminutive or "lower" character like a Neurotic, Slob or Nerd will give you the greatest Ironic contrast. If your story is small or centers around the meager existence of the characters, a grand Archetype like the Royal, the Leader, or the Hero will give you the greatest Ironic contrast. A good example of this practice in action is Pixar's *Ratatouille*. For a story set in the sophisticated circle of the finest chefs in Paris, they chose diminutive Archetypes, the Naif and the Fish Out of Water, for the lead character of Remy. They also made him a rat, resulting in extreme Irony. Remy is the exact opposite type of character you would expect to inhabit the world of the finest Paris chefs.

If you've already created a character but haven't come up with a story for them to inhabit, you can write a story based on a character once you know the character's Archetype. Build an environment around the character that gives you the same kind of comedic contrast. Only the most heightened contrast will create Irony and therefore comedy. For example, if you've developed a character who's primarily a Tough, putting that character in a soft, gentle environment will result in myriad opportunities for laughs. This was the path taken by the creators of *Kindergarten Cop*. They took an action-hero Archetype (a Fighter and a Tough) and put him in a kindergarten classroom.

WHERE JOKES COME FROM

Once you have a character and a story to put them in, the primary way you'll create jokes out of the pairing of the two is simply by using the Character Funny Filter, which means showing the character acting in accordance with their traits, as demonstrated in the movie scenes above. If you've laid the proper foundation, with an Archetype that contrasts with a good part of their environment, and then you show them acting in accordance with their traits, you've set the stage for laughs.

Archetypes for comedy characters should be thought of in the same way we think of the personalities of real people. People are all different, but there are certain recurring types, and we can often predict what certain people will do based on their personality types. Once your audience knows who your characters are, they'll expect them to behave in a certain way. This is the principle of the Character Funny Filter.

But just like real people aren't always restrained by their personalities, comedic characters don't have to be either.

Dramatist John Truby has a theory that all funny Character Archetypes represent humans descending into one of three different states: child, animal, or machine. Archetypes like the Grownup Child, the Jerk, or any type of character with overtly emotional traits, often have out-of-control emotions. These characters descend into a child state. The Animal, the Slob, the Lothario, and other characters who can't seem to constrain their beastly appetites or physical urges, are reduced to an animal state. Rational, unemotional characters like the Robot, the Bureaucrat, or the straight Everyperson who seem unaware that anything funny is going on, are reduced to a machine state.

However, many of the funny character Archetypes, like the Royal, the Leader, or the Hero, represent characters ascending to a higher state. Ascension can be played for humor just as much as descension. Laughs can always come from simply using the Character Funny Filter and showing such characters acting on their traits. This can go on as long as the story is moving forward. However individual joke beats or funny scenes can come from characters momentarily taking on slightly different characteristics.

A character can drop down or pop up into behavior that either amplifies or contrasts their Archetype.

When you amplify a character's traits, you use the Hyperbole Funny Filter. An Archetype with "lower" traits like a Spacenut or a Primitive, can be made even spacier or more primitive. A character with "higher" traits like a Traveling Angel or Royal can be made even more powerful or more uppity.

When Jeff Daniels is stuck in the bathroom with violent diarrhea in *Dumb and Dumber* he's already a funny character with "lower" traits (he's a Dummy). But now he's dropped into an even lower state, that of an animal, reduced to basic bodily functions, but only for one scene. This amplifies his traits using the Hyperbole and Shock Funny Filters to create additional layers of comedy.

When you contrast a character's behavior with their traits, you use Irony. For example, when a character is identified by the audience as a "lower" Archetype like an Animal or a Primitive, it can be incredibly funny when that character suddenly behaves like a Know-It-All or a Cool Cat briefly, periodically, or for an entire scene or episode, like when Homer Simpson became super smart (in the "HOMR" episode of *The Simpsons*), or when the Scarecrow got his brain at the end of *The Wizard of Oz*.

In the case of Homer Simpson, he ascends for a prolonged period, which creates an opportunity to write all kinds of new jokes previously unattainable with the regular Homer Simpson character. In the case of the Scarecrow, he pops into an ascended state for just one joke in the scene. You can drop down or pop up a character for as long or as briefly as you want, whichever gives you the best comedy.

When you use the Funny Filters to create Character Hyperbole in some scenes or moments and Character Irony in another, you create variety and layers of humor that make a fun ride for the audience.

Eddie Murphy was the Trickster in the opening of *Trading Places*, where he's introduced as a small-time street grifter. But as soon as he embarks on the journey of the movie, placed at the head of a large financial firm, he morphs into an Everyperson, seeing from the outside the crazy way the financial system runs. Suddenly he identifies more with the audience, deepening his bond with them. He's also, alternately, a Fish out of Water and a Hero. But in the film's climax, and in various moments throughout the film, he returns to his Trickster roots, and drops into other states as well to keep things fun and interesting.

While characters can morph from one Archetype into another within a story for comic effect, such moves can be complicated. They can confuse audiences if too frequent or handled clumsily, like if the Archetype isn't clearly defined from the start. Think of your character's Archetypal traits as an anchor so as not to confuse your audience. Once assigned a role, your character will set the expectations of the audience. They'll want your character to behave accordingly and always return to their default state. Being able to bend a character or move them fluidly through several Archetypes or Funny Filter-inspired drop downs or pop ups is a skill that comes with practice. To start working with characters, pick an Archetype, make it original, and let your audience get to know them. It's best to keep things simple, especially when you're just starting out writing comedy.

Once you're ready to experiment, you'll find that Irony and Hyperbole aren't the only Funny Filters you can use to build stories around characters or characters around stories. You can use the Shock, Misplaced Focus, Madcap, or Metahumor Filters as well. If you pair a Klutz with Madcap, you'll have a riotous physical comedy like *Naked Gun*. If you pair a Jerk with Misplaced Focus, you'll have a steady stream of funny situations like in *Despicable Me*. For a truly sophisticated level of humor in a story, try using the Analogy and Metahumor Funny Filters. With these advanced Filters, you can elevate your story to satirical heights. Experiment. Pair different Archetypes with different Funny Filters and you'll find an infinite variety of combinations, any one of which could result in blockbuster comedy entertainment.

COMIC RELIEF

Otherwise sober, dramatic stories often need a dose of humor. You can drop a character down into "lower" behavior or pop them up into "higher" behavior to add touches of humor to a serious story. These drop downs and pop ups are especially effective when the momentary behavior either contrasts their traits (with Irony), amplifies them (with Hyperbole), or engages other Funny Filters. For example, in *The King's Speech*, the normally dignified king descends into a childlike or animalistic state when he learns that he can overcome his stutter by swearing, so he unleashes a flood of swearwords. This employs the Shock and Irony Funny Filter, and instant comedy results.

Examine funny stories you like that use characters similar to the character you've created, in any medium. Learn to identify the Archetypes. Learn to articulate the contrast between the Archetype and their story environment. See if you can spot any other Funny Filters at work. You'll discover how writers weave Archetypes into their story, how they establish the character's traits, and how they play with the Funny Filters to create comedy. Analyze stories you don't like too. See why the ones you liked worked, and see why the ones you didn't like didn't work.

> FUNNY-CHARACTER TIP #6: CONTRAST YOUR CHARACTERS
>
> *Buddies, lovers, and popular comedy duos are almost always polar opposites: A Dummy and a Know-It-All, a Clown and an Everyperson, a Klutz and a Hero. But Archetypes aren't the only way to contrast characters. You can also symbolize their contrast and heighten their differences by contrasting their size, shape, sound, or manner. Penn was a loud talker, Teller was mute. Laurel was thin, Hardy was rotund. C3PO is full height, thin, gold, and fearful. R2-D2 is short, round, silver, and brave.*

If you look closely, another thing you'll notice besides all the comedy going on, is that Archetypes, especially ones in leading roles, have a one more special quality that has nothing to do with comedy, yet it's essential in any comedy story. You need to add this special spark of life to your characters. In the next chapter you'll get eight of the most reliable techniques to do it.

7

WHY SHOULD WE CARE?

In longer-form entertainment, your audience will lose interest in your character quickly if you don't imbue that character with one critical quality. Even if the character is funny enough to garner a couple of laughs from the audience in the first few minutes, the character will still fail if it lacks this one quality. Most storytellers fail in this regard, and it's why most stories, screenplays, and novels are just plain bad.

No, the characters don't have to be likable. That's not the quality that matters. "Your lead character needs to be more likable" is a Hollywood development cliché. Characters *can* be likable. That's not a bad thing. In fact, they usually are likable, even lovable. Getting your audience to fall in love with a character usually leads to great success. But it's not a requirement for your story. Audiences don't want to love every protagonist.

In fact, your protagonist can be as unlikable—as abhorrent—as you want, as long as you portray them properly, with the proper balance of positive and negative qualities. If your character fits into a traditionally unlikable Archetype, like the Jerk, the Bumbling Authority, the Psycho, or the Anti-Hero, the audience will expect them to be unlikable on some level. And you may be doing more harm than good by trying to make the audience like them. That's not the point with such characters. (See the Grinch, Rupert Pupkin, Walter White, and Phil Connors). The point is to get the audience to be either morbidly fascinated by them, intrigued by them, or at the very least interested in their fate. If you've determined that you don't want the audience to love your characters, then at least make the audience love to hate your characters. In all cases, a character only needs to accomplish one thing: to make the audience empathize with them.

Empathy is just as necessary in comedy as in drama. Even in the wackiest screwball comedies, the audience must care. They must care enough to willingly surrender to you and let your character take them on a ride. And this is not as easy as it may sound. You might be able to get them at least curious at first, but eventually you need to get them to emotionally invest in the outcome of your story.

FUNNY-CHARACTER TIP #7: YOUR AUDIENCE DOESN'T CARE

The safest assumption you can make when telling a funny story is that your audience doesn't care about your characters or what will happen to them. If you're a new writer, you might assume the opposite, that audiences will care deeply about your characters. This is a beginner's mistake. Writers love their own characters, so they figure, why wouldn't an audience love them too? That's not how the world works. You can't just walk up to someone on the street and expect them to like and trust you. The same goes with your story. You're asking a lot of an audience to invest in your characters and trust you to tell them an engaging story. Your job is to win them over. They won't care at all about your characters or your story until you do the necessary work of building empathy.

Characters in short comedy pieces like sketches, skits, or articles, don't necessarily need to inspire the audience to empathize with them, but it doesn't hurt. And even for a short piece, the audience must still be minimally invested in the outcome for the sketch to work.

HOW TO MAKE THE AUDIENCE CARE

There are several reliable techniques for making a character empathetic. These 8 are the most effective.

1. Make your character obsessively driven

In longer stories, this is not an optional technique. It's an essential quality that will make audiences at first curious enough to keep watching, reading, or listening to your story. As the story deepens, that curiosity should turn to interest, and then to fascination. For whatever reason, human beings are virtually incapable of averting their eyes when watching someone obsessively trying to achieve a clear objective, especially one that they consider worthy. What is your character driven to do? You need to be able to answer this question simply and clearly. Are they passionately driven? Would they do anything to keep pursuing their drive? You need to be able to answer *yes* to these questions, and show the audience this answer in your character's every action.

A character's drive is different from their want and their need. Most protagonists have both a want and a need, which are often contradictory. Their want is a superficial desire that will likely only be granted at a cost (often early in the movie). Their need is their central character flaw that has to be overcome. The reason they're going through your story is to correct their flaw. This is not often the case with perfect characters like Traveling Angels or Heroes, but it's true for most others. In *An American Pickle*, Seth Rogan's character has a simple want: to raise money to develop an app. He has a deeper need: to learn to embrace his roots and connect with his family. But his drive is altogether different. His drive is what propels the story, and by giving in to this drive, he'll achieve both his want and his need. This is how most comedy stories work. Seth Rogan's drive in *An American Pickle* is to introduce his newly revived great-grandfather to the 21st century.

The drive is often instigated by the inciting incident, the event that takes place early in your story that throws a wrench into you protagonist's life and leaves all their wants and needs seemingly in ruin. Your character's effort to cope with, overcome, or accept the new reality brought on by this Earth-shaking catalyst is what propels their drive. It's often at odds with their want and seemingly at odds with their need, or flaw. But in the end, it's exactly what they needed to correct their flaw.

As the writer, you have to know your character's want, need, and drive. And you must make every action your character undertakes be yet another attempt to pursue the outcome of their drive. This outcome can be anything. It can be to find something, destroy something, save something, uncover a truth—it doesn't matter. E.T.'s drive is to go home. The Dude's drive in *The Big Lebowski* is to be compensated for the damage done to his carpet. The stepbrothers' drive in *Stepbrothers* is to love each other despite the fact that they hate each other. The only two things that matter in regard to the drive are (1) that your character or characters are driven to do something that resolves your story satisfactorily, and (2) that the audience can get on board with it.

If your character is unlikeable, it's a good idea to give them a mission that's not only empathetic but sympathetic, something that redeems them and serves as a counter balance to their unlikable qualities. The low-life criminal Blues Brothers had to raise $5,000 to save an orphanage. The spoiled prince of Zamunda had to search America to find a bride who loved him for who he really is. Drug dealer Walter White had to support his wife, infant daughter, and disabled son.

2. Pit your character against impossible odds and/or a powerful antagonist

Whatever your character's want, need, or drive, they must face a powerful opposing force that's actively trying to stop them from achieving their desired outcome. Ideally, the opposing force (your story's antagonist) is trying to achieve the opposite outcome. E.T.'s antagonists, the government agents, want to prevent E.T. from going home. The Dude's antagonist, porn king Jackie Treehorn, continues to send henchmen to soil, steal, or otherwise prevent the Dude from being compensated for his damaged carpet. Each Stepbrother is the other's antagonist, making it impossible for them to coexist.

An antagonist doesn't have to be another person. It can be a phenomenon, like in *Groundhog Day* or *This is the End*. But it still must be a powerful and relentless force against your protagonist's drive.

In most cases the audience knows your characters will achieve the stated purpose of their drive by the end of your story, of course. But they want to see your characters struggle and fight against impossible odds to get there.

Who or what stands in your character's way? You must be able to answer this question specifically, and show the audience just how powerful that antagonistic force is.

3. Make your character relatable

When you make your character relatable, the audience steps into their shoes and automatically cares about them, no matter how likable or unlikeable your character may be. Suddenly they're an avatar for the audience, and the audience will be more likely to mirror your character's emotions. This is another way to make use of the Reference Funny Filter not just for laughs, but for emotional engagement in your story.

You may want your character to elicit a different emotion from your audience at different stages of your story. A common pattern is to elicit mystery and curiosity at first, since you're only just introducing the character—it's not easy to make an audience fall instantly in love. Once you've piqued their curiosity, you may want to make them like or understand your character. By the end of your story, you may want the audience to go to the ends of the Earth with your character. Whatever the case, you must be clear on how you want your audience to feel about your character at each stage of your story.

Showing your character doing something that the audience can relate to, or would do themselves if they were in a similar position, is a good way to pull your audience into the character, taking them from a feeling of curiosity to a feeling of familiarity and empathy. This technique is especially effective in science-fiction or fantasy comedies, where characters are in unusual or impossible settings. If the audience can identify with what's happening on a human level, they're more likely to suspend their disbelief and go along with the story.

Relatability can come in a sustained situation or in a single moment. In *Spy*, Melissa McCarthy's character, an Everyperson Archetype, wants to be recognized for doing a good job at work. This is a scenario most of us can relate to because we've all experienced such job-related anxiety ourselves. There's a masterful moment of engineered relatability in Alfred Hitchcock's *Psycho*. After Norman Bates cleans up the shower-murder scene by putting the victim's body in her car and pushing it into a murky swamp, the car gets almost all the way under the water's surface, but then sputters and stops, with a small section of the hood sticking up out of the water in clear view. The audience feels Norman's fear as he looks around, wondering how he's going to get the car to go all the way under the water. After this tense moment of uncertainty, there's one last bubbling sound, and the car sinks all the way down. Norman sighs in relief, and the audience sighs along with him. With this small, relatable, and funny moment, Hitchcock used the Reference Funny Filter to make audiences empathize with a deranged killer, and from that moment on, the master director had them in the palm of his hand.

4. Give your character positive qualities

There are hundreds of positive qualities you can give to a character that will make audiences empathize with them. They can be sweet, funny, loyal, thoughtful, brave—the list is endless. Any positive quality will serve to make your character more empathetic to the audience.

You still see some creators using the old pet-the-dog or pet-the-kitty technique, and that's because it works. When a character treats someone or something with kindness—especially someone or something that's weak or defenseless—it always wins over audiences and makes them want to invest in a character's journey, at least for a moment. Other techniques or more sustained good deeds will have to be employed to maintain that investment. The better writers give this old technique a twist and don't simply show their characters walking past a dog and petting it. They achieve the same effect in more inventive ways.

First, they integrate story exposition, so any kindness the character shows to a random helpless animal will also further the story by showing the character pursuing their want (prior to the inciting incident) or their drive (after the inciting incident).

Second, they make it unique. In *Feed the Kitty*, the classic *Looney Tunes* short, a mammoth bulldog confronts a tiny, adorable kitten, attempting to terrorize it with his aggressive posture and ferocious bark. The kitten is unphased by the dog's boisterous threats, and instead of running away in fear, she nonchalantly saunters up his arm and onto his back, kneads him with her claws, and then settles into his fur and goes to sleep. The dog's heart melts, and so does the audience's. In just a little over one minute into the movie, director Chuck Jones made the audience fall in love with both characters.

In *Rocky*, Adrien gives Rocky a gift from the pet store where she works: Butkus the dog. This gift furthered the love story subplot between Rocky and Adrien. The scenes with Butkus worked particularly well because Stallone and the dog had a moving backstory that audiences didn't even know about, but that enhanced the scene and created powerful empathy for Rocky. Before making the movie, when Stallone was out of work and destitute, he sold his dog for rent money, which broke his heart. After he got his lucky break and sold his script for *Rocky* and got it into production, he was able to buy the dog back and feature it in the movie. His deep, emotional connection with Butkus shines through on the screen.

5. Make your character the victim of undeserved misfortune

Undeserved misfortune is a powerful way to make audiences empathize with a character. Bill Murray's life falls apart at the beginning of *Stripes*. He loses his job, his apartment, and his girlfriend. Charlie Brown and other Sadsack characters use the undeserved-misfortune technique not only in the beginning of a story to rope audiences in, but perpetually, to keep audiences feeling more and more sorry for them.

Chuck Jones adds an escalating dose of undeserved misfortune to the bulldog in *Feed the Kitty*. The dog has to conceal his new pet kitten and protect it from his cruel owner, who constantly berates and beats him, which makes the audience fall even more deeply in love with him.

Chuck Jones used the same technique repeatedly with Wile E. Coyote, using his trait as the Klutz Archetype. He's bested every time by the Road Runner while suffering undeserved, Madcap misfortune.

This technique can even work to engender empathy for extremely unlikeable characters, such as when the Dukes take away all of Royal Archetype Dan Aykroyd's wealth and privilege in *Trading Places*. He suffers such humiliating misfortune that the audience can't help but empathize with him.

6. Put your character in a low station in society

If your character is a homeless person, a prisoner, a slave, an outcast, an abused pet, a neglected baby, or a character with any kind of down-and-out station in life, your audience will be more inclined to empathize with them. If your character faces impossible odds on top of such a low station, audiences will root for them even more.

C3PO and R2-D2 took advantage of this technique in *Star Wars*, a world where droids were second-class citizens at the bottom of the galaxy's social hierarchy. This positioned them well to be among the film's most relatable and funny characters, the ones who took the audience through all the films in the series.

7. Show other characters demonstrating their feelings for your character

This is a more superficial technique, but it still works. It works especially well as a way to introduce a character. You can encourage audiences to feel a certain way about a character before they meet them if you show other characters having the same feeling about them. It's a way to give your character a reputation to live up to. If you want audiences to be intrigued by a character, show other characters being intrigued. If you want them to be intimidated, show other characters intimidated, and so on.

This simple technique goes a long way to encouraging the right kind of empathetic response you want in your audience.

In *Casablanca*, people speak of Humphrey Bogart's character Rick with a sense of curiosity and mystery before he's introduced. In the opening of *Citizen Kane*, a grandiose newsreel narrator tells the larger-than-life story of Charles Foster Kane, and then other characters try to unravel the mystery of the man and the significance of his last word, "Rosebud." Obi Wan Kenobi is introduced with this technique in *Star Wars*.

You can even use this technique to encourage your audience to love your characters. This was used to set up the character of Mary in *There's Something About Mary*, and Ariel in *The Little Mermaid*. If you can show other characters acting in a way that demonstrates that they love your character, the audience will be predisposed to love them too.

The same goes, of course, for characters you want the audience to hate. If you show how these characters' bad behavior or outright evil affects the other characters, the audience will be inclined to hate them. If other characters hate your character unjustly, the audience will read it as undeserved misfortune. If a character's hatred is deserved, the audience will be intrigued and want to meet this terrible character. This can be a delicious way to introduce a comedy villain, or a protagonist who fits into a naturally unlikeable or love-to-hate Archetype like a Jerk or Anti-Hero.

The important thing to remember with this technique is that your character should always live up to the hype. Ideally, you want to overdeliver on the audience's expectations.

8. Make your character the least evil

Some story settings are made up of nothing but despicable characters. Stories about mobsters, prisoners, or demons often fall into this category. Stirring up feelings of empathy for such overtly evil characters may seem like a daunting task, but it's actually quite easy. Simply make your lead character, or any character you want the audience to empathize with, the least evil character in the bunch. Audiences will gravitate to that character like they would a lifeline, and make it the repository for their empathy. Adam Sandler used this technique in *Little Nicky*.

With evil characters, you may find it necessary to use not just one or two of these empathy-engineering techniques, but several, one on top of the other. You might need to fire every weapon in your arsenal to make audiences care. *Little Nicky* uses almost all of the techniques in this chapter to make audiences care about the lead character.

- He's passionately driven with an empathetic goal
- He faces impossible opponents (two older demon brothers)
- He's continuously relatable (learning to be a human living on Earth)
- He has positive qualities: He's the kindest of Satan's three sons. He even befriends a dog (a possessed dog, but still a dog, making this clichéd technique feel original)
- He suffers undeserved misfortune, being disfigured from abuse and tormented by his brothers
- He occupies a low station, both in his family and in Earth society
- Another character develops feelings for him and falls in love with him
- He's the least evil character among the demons

Any one of these techniques can work for your character. You may find a combination of several works best. Depending on the type of character you're working with, you may only need to use these techniques as breadcrumbs, to subtly suggest that your audience empathize with your character. But most of them time you'll need to hit audiences over the head. Remember that they don't care, and it's your job as the writer to make them care.

Practice and feedback from others will help you find the right amount of empathy building you'll need.

Another important step you can take toward making sure your characters connect with audiences is to avoid the 9 most common funny-character mistakes detailed in the next chapter.

8

THE 9 MOST COMMON CHARACTER MISTAKES

Most funny characters written by amateurs fall flat. Here are the 9 most common reasons why, in order of the most common. Where possible, examples of these mistakes are listed. However, most stories that make these mistakes die before they ever get produced, which makes produced and released examples hard to find.

1. The writer uses funny lines to make a funny character

The biggest mistake writers make when trying to write funny characters is to rely on written gags for laughs instead of trusted funny Character Archetypes. Worse, these gags are often at odds with the character's traits.

With very few exceptions, humor in a story comes from the characters acting in accordance with their established traits (using the Character Funny Filter) while propelling the story forward on the track of the character's drive. Any spoken gag that doesn't meet these two requirements will not only fail as an attempt to get laughs, it will torpedo the project. Audiences will lose interest and look elsewhere for entertainment.

Lines of dialogue should be the last thing the writer of a story thinks about or worries about. If a novel, screenplay or stage play were a house, the written lines of dialogue would be doilies placed on top of furnishings long after the house has been built, painted, and furnished. When a writer tries to write funny lines to propel a story, they might as well be draping doilies over weeds in an empty lot.

Once you have a compelling story populated with character Archetypes, and you know how those characters will act in any situation, simply write their dialogue to be true to their character, and laughs will result.

One of the funniest lines in the movie *Zoolander* comes when Ben Stiller's character Derek Zoolander (the Dummy Archetype), gets upset with Mustafa's miniature model for his proposed "Derek Zoolander Center for Kids Who Can't Read Good":

```
                    DEREK ZOOLANDER
          What is this?

     He smashes model on the floor.

                    DEREK ZOOLANDER (CONT'D)
          A center for ants!?

                    MUSTAFA
          What?

                    DEREK ZOOLANDER
          How can we be expected to teach children
          to learn how to read if they can't even
          fit inside the building?
```

The only reason this exchange is funny is because it shows a Dummy, acting like a Dummy, and it deepens the stakes in the story, complicating Mustafa's attempt to brainwash and control Zoolander. It's not any kind of traditional gag with a setup and punchline. By itself, it barely makes sense as a joke. It only works in the context of the characters and the story.

Movies like *Buckaroo Banzai* and *Space Sweepers* are examples of movies that try to rely on funny lines to make characters funny.

2. The writer tries to think of funny things for the character to do

A lot of writers have learned, rightly, that it's action that makes a character, not lines of dialogue. They therefore think characters need to act crazy or do outrageous, funny things in order to be funny. But these things alone will only serve to alienate audiences. Characters only need to act in accordance with their traits and drive the story. Your best route to get laughs is to plot your story well, chose good Archetypes for your characters, and then show them acting on their traits in order to move the story forward.

For a comedic story, it helps to have Irony at the core, with built-in contrast with your character. In *Hot Tub Time Machine*, four guys dissatisfied with their lives are forced to relive them. In *Beverly Hills Cop*, Eddie Murphy is a rough and tumble cop from inner-city Detroit suddenly policing one of the most posh communities in the world. In almost every great comedy movie, you'll find this kind of Irony, a plot or setting that is the polar opposite from what you would expect your characters to inhabit.

This Irony is largely what creates sustained comedy in longer stories. When you have Character Archetypes driving forward and acting on their traits on top of the Irony, you don't need to think of random funny things the characters can do for laughs. What makes funny action is simply showing them moving through the story doing what their character would do to achieve their goal or solve the problem of the inciting incident.

For a dramatic story, you're likely dealing with a single comedic scene or a single comic relief character. The same principles apply. Make sure you have Irony or another Funny Filter inherent in the scene, and "drop" an otherwise dramatic character into a two-dimensional Archetype for the duration of the scene or moment.

In Quentin Tarantino's *Django Unchained*, the horse-raid scene with the Ku Klux Klan is set up with tremendous Irony. He introduces the intimidating horde with dramatic shots of galloping masked horsemen carrying torches accompanied by epic choir music. But when the men speak, they drop into Dummy and Klutz Archetypes, unable to see through their masks or agree on whether the masks are a good idea. Tarantino uses the Reference Funny Filter (with the Klansmen having normal conversations we all recognize about coordinating a gathering), and the Shock Funny Filter (with liberal swearing) to add even more humor to the scene, mocking the Klansmen as incompetent goofs.

In Jordan Peele's *Get Out*, the comic relief character, Rob, is the Every-person Archetype. His down-to-Earth assessments of the situation contrast perfectly with the outlandish sci-fi human-trafficking plot. His job at the TSA provides further Ironic contrast, representing the smallest and least effective law enforcement agency one would hope to engage to stop such a terrible plot. To get laughs, all he needs to do is act like an Every-person—to say the obvious things that the audience is thinking.

Fred: The Movie is an example of a story where the main character does silly things to get laughs instead of contrasting with his environment and creating genuine Irony.

> FUNNY-CHARACTER TIP #8: AVOID STEREOTYPES
>
> *The worst examples of clichéd characters are those who aren't even Archetypes. Characters like the hooker with the heart of gold, the absent-minded professor, or the abusive boyfriend/husband. Worse still are ethnic or racial stereotypes like the Indian shopkeeper (which The Simpsons finally retired) or the angry Black youth. Avoid these characters at all costs. These are stereotypes, not Archetypes.*

3. The character is clichéd

Sometimes writers have just enough knowledge to be dangerous. They know and understand the Character Archetypes, but they don't take the important additional step of making them unique. As a result, their characters come off as tired and uninteresting, mere carbon copies of characters we've seen countless times before.

The 40s private eye is a character that's been trotted out too many times. The only way to make it fresh is to use one of the techniques in Chapter 5, like Frank Miller did in *Sin City*, or Steve Martin in *Dead Men Don't Wear Plaid*. *The Cheap Detective* was an attempt to parody the detective genre. But it failed to make this clichéd character unique, and as a result it's a virtually unwatchable star-studded movie.

A clichéd Archetype actually has a prayer of working with audiences if enough time has passed since the audience last saw that Archetype, or if the story is compelling enough. For example, the Princess in *The Princess Bride* is a standard Royal, but the story she's in is unique enough, and she's surrounded by so many other unique Archetypes, the overall effect is positive.

4. The dialogue doesn't sparkle

If a Character Archetype is properly chosen to provide Ironic contrast with the plot, setting, or other characters, the dialogue should practically write itself. As explained above, dialogue is the last thing a good writer should worry about. However, if a writer happens to be good at constructing stories and characters but has a tin ear for dialogue, it's worth pointing out this common mistake.

Many amateur, unproduced screenplays suffer from flat dialogue, which is usually an indication that the larger creative elements in the script (like character and plot) will also be flat. Dialogue is one of the first things a script reader sees, of course, so they naturally assume that bad dialogue means a bad script, and they often stop reading before the end of page one.

Great dialogue in a bad story is rare. But such a dichotomy will at least keep someone hooked for a few pages. Eventually, however, no matter how amazing the dialogue, the deeper problems of poorly constructed characters and plots will remain.

Dialogue doesn't sparkle when the characters speak too "on the nose," without symbolism, subtext, or double meaning. Or worse, each character's dialogue is indistinguishable from the other characters. Kevin Smith movies often suffer from this problem, especially *Clerks*, the low-budget independent film that launched his career. The dialogue in many Kevin Smith movies sounds more like Kevin Smith than it does any fictional character.

Techniques for making dialogue pop off the page are coming in chapter 10.

5. The character doesn't want anything

A lead character can't be passive, but unfortunately too many stories can blame a passive lead character for their failure to hold an audience's attention. Characters come alive when they want something specific and pursue it obsessively. Too many amateur stories are about people sitting around talking. Don't ever write a story like that. No one is interested in it. Audiences want to see characters going on a journey or a quest, and they want to see them struggle to achieve whatever it is they're driven to achieve.

Some successful stories have passive main characters, but it's extremely rare. One example is Richard Linklater's *Boyhood*. It's worth noting that a story like this requires advanced storytelling skill, and Linklater is one of the few masters of the craft. Such stories are often structured as Unity of Place or Unity of Time stories as opposed to the far more common Unity of Action story. I recommend any beginning storyteller start with a Unity of Action story, which makes up 99.99 percent of all stories told. Aristotle broke down these three kinds of stories in his seminal book on story structure, *Poetics*. I provide guidelines for how a modern comedy writer can use these three stories in *How to Write Funnier*.

Still, some characters in Unity of Action stories are passive. It's not easy to accomplish. Arthur Dent and Harry Potter are prominent examples. These characters more often experience things happening to them, as opposed to them driving the action. Note how the writers solve this problem by giving the characters strong desires at the very least, and short-term practical goals to achieve even if they are more of a cog as opposed to the prime movers in the overall story. They also use other tricks like making the story about something bigger, something epic. The structure of the story in *The Hitchhiker's Guide to the Galaxy* is more about the discovery of the universe than of any personal journey by the protagonist. We experience the wacky universe through Arthur Dent's eyes. The many books in the Harry Potter series are similar. We're introduced to the world of Hogwarts through Harry Potter.

Don't confuse inert for passive. Jimmy Stewart's character in Alfred Hitchcock's *Rear Window* may be confined to a wheelchair in his apartment for the entire movie, but he's in passionate pursuit of clues about the murder he suspects in the apartment across the way. The "Three O'Clock" episode of the radio show *Suspense,* which features a man tied to a chair and gagged for the entire episode, is a master class in how to write a riveting inert character. He is anything but passive.

If you're a beginner, don't try to be fancy. Make your character active. Make sure your character wants something and will do anything to get it.

6. The character isn't extreme enough

In a lot of comedy stories that don't work, the characters' journey isn't big enough, their actions are too subtle, or the contrast between them and the plot, setting, or other characters, isn't heightened enough.

For a TV episode or a short story, or even a stage play, characters can afford to embark on extremely small journeys, but for a movie or novel, whatever's happening to your main character should be the most remarkable event in their life. You need a level of spectacle worthy of the medium. In amateur stories, characters often have common, uninteresting, or pedestrian adventures, like losing a friend, starting a business, or planning an event. These things are not big enough for a movie or novel.

Another mistake a lot of amateur humor writers make is creating a character with poorly defined traits, or traits that are too subtle. Even with an Archetype, a character's traits have to be obvious to the audience or it won't be funny. How can you tell if your character's traits are obvious enough? It's almost impossible to be too extreme with a funny character. In most cases, the more extreme your character, the funnier it will be. But a simple method for determining if the traits are extreme enough is to make sure people laugh when the character acts in accordance with their traits. For example, if you're using a Robot Archetype, when that character reacts in a deadpan way to some extremely emotional event, your audience should recognize it as a joke. If they don't, you're probably portraying it too subtly. Test your writing on an audience of beta-readers to make sure you're character's actions are extreme enough.

The worst sin a writer can commit with a character, and one that's guaranteed to make for flat, uninteresting, and unfunny characters, is to fail to assign an Archetype. In *The Love Guru,* Mike Meyers failed to assign an

Archetype to his main character. He had great success with Austin Powers as the Lothario Archetype, which was a natural fit for *The Love Guru*, but perhaps in his desire to distinguish the two characters, he missed an obvious opportunity. The Love Guru is almost a Know-It-All, but his traits aren't clear.

If your protagonist has no definable traits, they're not an Archetype. And if you have other characters in your story with similarly ill-defined traits, all your characters will blend together. They'll feel the same, and the audience will be left grasping for any characteristics they can identify with in order to care about what's happening. In these kinds of stories, the audience isn't hooked. They could leave the story at any point and not feel like they missed out. *The Fifth Element* is a movie like this.

7. There's too much character description

One of the most important rules of writing any kind of fiction is "Show, don't tell." Amateur scriptwriters often write several lines of description for a character, especially a main character, before that character is introduced or has spoken a single line of dialogue. This is a waste of time. In novels, pages and pages about a character's appearance or backstory are just as useless.

Seasoned readers are skipping over all that description. They know that it's action that makes a character, not description.

An experienced script reader knows that a lot of that description is probably backstory or exposition, which the audience of the resulting film or TV show doesn't know yet. Therefore, it's irrelevant and shouldn't be conveyed to the reader. The only thing the end audience will see is what the character looks like and does. A short line or two is all that's necessary to describe a character. The rest will be shown through the character's actions. What they do will be far more impactful than how you describe them.

Look at the way two famous Trickster Archetypes are introduced: In *Willy Wonka & the Chocolate Factory*, Willy Wonka emerges from the chocolate factory as a slow and feeble old man, barely able to limp along with his cane. He begins to fall flat on his face, but then summersaults at the last second and pops into a triumphant, welcoming pose. In *Pirates of the Caribbean*, Jack Sparrow comes ashore on a sinking sailboat just before it disappears in the water, walking from the top of the mast onto the dock without missing a step. These wordless tricks tell you more about these clear Character Archetypes in a single moment than any long scene of description ever could.

8. The writer doesn't compel the audience to care about the character

As illustrated in the previous chapter, there are several easy techniques for making an audience empathize with a funny character. But most writers fail to do this work. They assume people will naturally like their characters, sympathize with them, and be interested in their journey. But they're not. The audience is pre-disposed to be uninterested, and it's the writer's job to attract them, hook them, and reel them in. It takes a little extra work and a lot of thought to create the proper balance of empathy in any kind of character, but it's an essential step that can't be skipped.

9. The writer doesn't understand the difference between comedic and dramatic characters

Comedic Characters are not the same as dramatic characters, and dramatic characters are not the same as comedic characters. They are, in fact, a world apart. They serve entirely different functions in a story. When a writer fails to understand this, they confuse their audience about the genre of their story. And confusion is the enemy of comedy.

This mistake is more complicated than the others here, so the entire next chapter lays out the differences between comedic and dramatic characters, and how to make each one work for your story.

9

COMEDIC CHARACTERS vs. DRAMATIC CHARACTERS

In Aristotle's time, two central classifications of storytelling were comedy and tragedy. He defined them by saying comedy represents people as worse than real life, and tragedy represents people as better than real life. A third class of story, epic, was what he called poems like *The Iliad* and *The Odyssey*. Epic is largely akin to tragedy as opposed to comedy.

What Aristotle called a comedy would comprise the vast majority of stories told today. There are very few modern tragedies. In the capitalistic entertainment business of the modern world, there's not much room for tragedy because it doesn't sell as many tickets as comedy. Oedipus Rex killing his father, having sex with his mother, and then gouging his own eyes out is not exactly hit box-office material.

Science fiction, superhero, spy thrillers, and other seemingly dramatic stories are used as examples throughout this book because they are, in the strictest sense, Aristotelian comedies.

Aristotle's definitions and story classifications were evolving when he wrote about them 2000 years ago, and they continue to evolve today. In our time, the entertainment business also divides stories into two primary categories, but they're not comedy and tragedy. They're comedy and drama. Comedies are the stories meant to make us laugh, and dramas are the stories meant to make us cry. Dramas encompass tragic and epic stories. Comedies encompass everything else, including most horror, science fiction, and fantasy—anything meant to be fun. Dramas win the Academy Award for Best Picture. Comedies almost never do.

For the modern storyteller, this classification is important for one key reason: the way characters are treated in dramas as opposed to comedies is as different as day and night.

A dramatic story is any story depicting action the audience is meant to perceive the same as they would real life, with a full range of emotional responses, and with the expectation that the characters will be realistic or believable. Drama is expected to be a faithful representation of reality.

Dramatic characters are meant to be complex, nuanced, and contradictory. Audiences want living, breathing, flesh-and-blood characters in a drama. To write a dramatic character, a writer often writes several paragraphs of backstory, describing the character's upbringing, family history, what they ate for breakfast this morning, and all the details about their tortured past. In the best-selling novel *Jaws*, the source material for Steven Spielberg's classic movie, author Peter Benchley even bothered to describe how Sheriff Brody pees.

The audience of a drama wants all that. They want to get inside the head of a dramatic character and experience them in three dimensions like they would a person in the real world. To suspend their disbelief, they need to feel that everything happening in a drama could be real. Many dramas are based on true stories after all. In *The Dallas Buyer's Club*, we witness the realistic consequences of the actions of Matthew McConaughey and Jared Leto's characters in ways we would never expect in a comedy.

Comedy, on the other hand, doesn't need any of that. Comedy is any work of entertainment the audience is meant to treat not like real life, but like life through a funhouse mirror. Comedy is an artist's crazy interpretation of real life, where one central thing is off kilter, and things don't work quite the same way as they do in the real world. Audiences don't expect the characters in a comedy be believable, flesh-and-blood people. They expect them to be mere symbols, or two-dimensional representations of people. They're us, but through the funhouse mirror.

To make a comedic character, you don't need to write their elaborate history or know their psychological profile (unless you need to know facts about their history for plot points). You only need to pick an Archetype and then show them acting in accordance with the Archetype's traits while they're driving the story.

> FUNNY-CHARACTER TIP #9: AVOID CLICHÉD SPEECH
>
> *If you've heard certain lines or even patterns of speech in fiction before, don't repeat it. There are so many subtle ways that clichés can sneak into dialogue without writers realizing it. Conventions that we take for granted are best discarded in favor of an all-new approach. Let your characters speak in such a distinctive way that they sound like no one else.*

MIXING COMEDY AND DRAMA

Adding a touch of drama to a comedy story or a touch of comedy to a dramatic story spices up stories and keeps audiences engaged. But such crossovers have to be handled carefully. It's not as easy as it looks.

You can take a comedy character out of a comedy world and put them in a dramatic story. This happens frequently. These characters are called comic relief characters. The way comic relief characters work in dramatic stories is the same way they work in comedy stories: they should be an Archetype, and they should use the Character Funny Filter to get laughs by behaving in accordance with their traits.

Even straight dramatic characters can be funny in a dramatic story.

All they need to do to become comedic is drop into a two-dimensional Archetype in line with one or more of the Funny Filters for a moment or a short scene. Audiences enjoy seeing an otherwise serious and believable character take a brief, funny turn.

But you can't put a dramatic character in a comedy story. It won't work. If you take Meryl Streep from *Sophie's Choice* and try to place her in any kind of comedy movie, the worlds would collide and they would both fall apart.

The only way to add drama to a comedy story is to find some pathos in your existing comedy Archetype. Your Archetype won't suddenly become a flesh-and-blood character meant to be accepted as a real person. They'll still be a two-dimensional comedy representation. But they can display what passes for genuine emotion in their comedy world, which most often means a far more exaggerated emotional reaction than a real person's. Or they can have a realistic emotional reaction to something in the story based on a comedy-world scenario that couldn't possibly happen in real life. They can even have a realistic emotional reaction to a realistic event. In all cases, they remain a character Archetype momentarily showing emotion, and nothing more. They don't become a realistic character. For example, a Tough like Nicolas Cage's character in *Raising Arizona* can have a touching emotional moment by returning the baby he kidnapped, symbolizing his transformation from criminal to law-abiding citizen. A Cool Cat-Lothario like John Candy in *Splash* can suddenly break down and admit that he's lonely and sad. These dramatic moments deepen the comedy, but this is the deepest you dare go in a comedy. Anything more realistic and dramatic will confuse audiences.

But let's say you've constructed an excellent, reality-based comedy story that has no zany, outlandish, or sci-fi elements. It's not *Groundhog Day* or *Freaky Friday*. It's more of a romantic-comedy like *Forgetting Sarah Marshall*, where the basic rules of reality are followed. And let's say your protagonist is an Everyperson who has real, natural reactions to the story. Isn't that a dramatic character? Won't the audience accept that character as "real"?

No. That character is still a comedic character and not a dramatic one. They're a mere funhouse representation of a real person. They can't transcend the comedy genre because, as part of that genre, they exist in a comedy world. Although there may not be a fantastical element that makes that particular comedy world wildly different from the real world, there's always something askew in a comedy world. At the very least, the characters behave in a more extreme, cartoonish, or unrealistic way than they would in the real world or in a dramatic story.

Furthermore, comedy characters accept the comedy world as their reality. They obey its rules. Outside of their world, they're lost. You can put a comedic character in a dramatic movie as the comic relief character because they would then accept the dramatic world as their reality and obey its rules. Comedic characters are trapped in whatever world they're in, comedic or dramatic. Dramatic characters are not trapped. They exist in a world just like ours.

"Dramedy" is a term for a story that purportedly weaves comedy and drama, but don't be fooled. All dramedies are comedies. TV shows like *M*A*S*H* and movies like *Juno* exist in impossible comedy worlds, where outlandish things happen and the characters are capable of brilliant witticisms. The worlds of such shows are idealized, hyperbolized, or otherwise skewed. They're decidedly different from ours.

Knowing how to balance comedic elements and dramatic elements for the most pleasing mix takes practice to master, and the proper balance is going to be different for every story. Therefore there's no one-size-fits-all formula. It's best to establish your genre clearly from the start of your story to orient the audience, and then, if you decide you need to veer into one or the other (comedy or drama), do so sparingly. You don't want to confuse audiences by making them wonder what your genre is. Audiences need to know whether something is meant to be real and believable as opposed to comedic and made-up. It's the writer's job to make the audience understand and accept whatever world they're in.

How do you establish your comedy world and introduce it to an audience? One major way is through the characters' dialogue. In the next chapter, you'll find the number one way to get your characters to say funny things.

10

'I'M TALKING' HERE!'

Your character's dialogue is one of the first things readers see. But don't write it. Not yet, anyway. Let your characters write it for you.

Remember that dialogue is just the trimmings. Your story structure and clear, well-chosen Archetypes who propel themselves through your story are the engine that keeps readers turning pages. If your story is poorly structured and your characters are uninteresting, your dialogue will bore audiences, no matter how clever or dazzling it might be.

Figure out your story structure first. This is where 99 percent of stories fail. Write out every major plot point of your story in a two-page prose treatment. Then, read that two-page treatment to a select group of beta-readers and ask them if they like it. They likely won't. Ask them where they lost interest and why. Ask them what they thought was going to happen. Ask them what they wished had happened. You'll probably rewrite this two-page treatment dozens of times. But that's easier than rewriting a 120-page screenplay or 300-page novel. Relish this easy process if you want to be in the 1 percent of stories that succeed.

Eventually, as you continue sharing this ever-evolving two-page treat-ment, you'll work out the story bugs. And people might start saying things like, "That's a great story," "I'd see that movie," or "I didn't want it to end!" When you get those kinds of reactions, you're ready to write out the full story, whether as a full-length script or novel.

Write your first draft quickly, in a month or less. Dash it off and don't worry about writing good dialogue. The time for dialogue will come dur-ing your second draft. Write a bunch of "on the nose" dialogue as a place-holder just to get the story beats down. You'll likely discover more story problems at this stage and you'll need to rewrite even more before you add any finishing touches.

Once beta-readers tell you your full-length story is working, then and only then go back and write your dialogue. By now, you'll know your characters and you'll know their journey. If you've chosen the right Ar-chetypes to fit your story, you'll have a good idea who they are and how they would talk. And they'll be dying to say something.

This process is the best way to write good dialogue.

What does this dialogue look like? It looks like this in the first draft:

```
                    JOHN
        Will you go to the park with me?
                    JANE
        Okay.
```

Or, if you're writing a novel, it looks like this:

"Will you go to the park with me?" John asked.
"Okay," Jane said.

That's the kind of flat, uninspiring dialogue that you want in a first draft of anything. It's too early to spend time perfecting dialogue at that stage. Before your story is worked out, any scenes you write now will likely be cut or changed. If you write some lines of dialogue that you think are brilliant, you'll resist cutting it, and your effort to write a good story will run aground. You won't be able to stomach killing your darlings. Don't make extra work for yourself. Your only goal with a first-draft is to get the story on the page, no matter how rough.

After you have your story figured out, go back and polish your description and improve these lines of dialogue. This will be your second draft. Your Archetypes will know just what to say. Let's suppose you've decided to make John a Lovable Scoundrel and Jane a Clown. Their dialogue would now look like this:

```
            JOHN
I want to see your pretty ass in some
nature.

            JANE
Pffft.
```

The same information is being communicated as before, but this time the Character Funny Filter has been employed, with each character acting in accordance with their Archetype. Other Funny Filters are used too, like Irony (with Jane seeming to derisively reject John's invitation) and Shock (with John's use of "ass," his brazenly familiar way of speaking to her, and her raspberry). We sense these two have a history.

Or let's say you decided to make John a Dummy-Naif hybrid and Jane a Know-It-All.

```
            JOHN
Would you, I dunno, want to go . . .
outdoors with me. Ever?

            JANE
Oxygen molecules in the lungs. Superb
suggestion. Not the sub-intellect you
appear to be, are you?
```

Whatever your Archetypes, the lines will now leap off the page. They're fresh. They make the reader curious about who these people are and what they might do next. And that's the goal in the beginning of any story. No jokes or gags or "clever dialogue" needs to be written. The only dialogue writing method the skilled comedy writer employs is choosing good

Archetypes that contrast with each other and the comedy world around them.

If your Archetypes fit your story and drive it, and the dialogue stays in character, you'll dig your hooks into the reader deeper with every page.

By practicing using Archetypes and making them drive stories, you get upstream of any dialogue-writing problems. Your characters will tell your story, as it should be.

But for good measure, here are some additional funny-dialogue writing tips:

1. Don't cast a celebrity

One tip a lot of writers recommend is to imagine a famous actor playing your character. As you write, you'll get inspired imagining what your character might say because they'll be coming not from you, but from the mouth of the imagined celebrity you've cast. Don't use this method. The dialogue you get from imagining a famous actor will be bland or typecast at best. The dialogue will be reminiscent of dialogue we've heard before. You'll get much fresher dialogue by picking a clear Archetype instead, and then imagining what your unique Archetype would say. And their dialogue will be far better suited to your unique story.

2. Make sure everyone sounds different

With contrasting Archetypes in your lead roles, you can be assured that the characters will sound markedly different from each other. Good dialogue in a novel doesn't need attribution. The reader should be able to tell who's talking just by the distinct way they're talking or what they're talking about. Hollywood script readers often don't read description or character attribution. They only read dialogue. If the characters are different enough, the reader can still follow your story.

Every character should have their own vocabulary, their own pet words, their own accent, their own speaking peculiarities, and their own sentence structure, like in this scene from the Cohen Brothers' *The Ladykillers*:

```
                         DORR
          I thank you, madam, for your act of
          kindness.
```

```
                    MRS. MUNSON
          Well you let him out.

                    DORR
          I certainly did and I do apologize no
          end. Allow me to present myself, uh,
          formally: Goldthwait Higginson Dorr,
          Ph.D.

                    MRS. MUNSON
          What, like Elmer?

                    DORR
          Beg your pardon, ma'am?

                    MRS. MUNSON
          Fudd?

                    DORR
          No no, Ph.D. is a mark of academic
          attainment. It is a degree of higher
          learning bestowed, in my case, in
          recognition of my mastery of the antique
          languages of Latin and Greek. I also hold
          a number of other advanced degrees
          including the baccalaureate from a school
          in Paris, France, called the Sorbonne.
```

Munson chuckles.

```
                    MRS. MUNSON
          Sore bone, well I guess that's
          appropriate. You ever study at Bob Jones
          University?

                    DORR
          I have not had that privilege.

                    MRS. MUNSON
          It's a bible school, only the finest in
          the country. I send them five dollars
          every month.

                    DORR
          That's very gener--

                    MRS. MUNSON
          I'm on their mailing list. I'm an Angel.

                    DORR
          Indeed.
```

3. Don't write superfluous dialogue

Whenever your characters talk, they should be both propelling your story and manifesting their traits. They should never talk just to talk.

4. Parody the way real people talk

Parody is yet another Funny Filter that can serve you well in dialogue writing. Listen to real people talking and try to borrow patterns of speech you hear. Lampoon it. When you apply real-world speaking styles to fictional characters, the effect can be powerful. Your dialogue will achieve a new level of quality when audiences recognize it on a subliminal level as dialog that seems more natural and less written.

5. Integrate exposition

Any "business" that you feel needs to be explained probably doesn't need to be. Unanswered questions and mysteries are the breadcrumbs that keep readers reading. Withhold more information than you reveal, and only give it out at the last possible moment. And always (except at the end), raise more questions to keep the reader guessing. When you finally have to explain anything or answer a question, reveal it in action. Don't do an "information dump."

6. Don't write gags

Instead of telling funny jokes or gags to make comedy dialogue, allow your characters to be themselves. Their lines will create all the humor by simply being in character. The Character Funny Filter will do its work, and as the opportunity arises, you can incorporate other Funny Filters as well, to drop characters down or pop them up.

7. Use subtext

It's far more interesting when characters communicate subtextually. The "on the nose" dialogue of your first draft is your subtext. At the second draft stage, rewrite your dialogue to convey this subtext without actually saying it. Let the audience add two and two to arrive at what the characters are really saying.

Here's an example of subtext in *The King of Comedy*:

```
                    JERRY
          How would the audience like to see the
          king of comedy marry his queen right here
          on the show?

The audience applauds.

                    RUPERT
          I can't believe this. I don't know what
          to say!

Rupert stands and hugs Jerry. He hugs fellow guest Dr.
Joyce Brothers, too. Jerry hugs back. It becomes a
comical hug fest.

Victor Borge plays the bridal chorus on the studio piano.

The stage curtain pulls back to reveal an elaborate
church set.
```

```
Rita and Rupert stand before Rupert's former High School
Principal, with Jerry and Dr. Joyce Brothers to the side.
                    HIGH SCHOOL PRINCIPAL
          Dearly beloved, when Rupert here was a
          student at the Clifton High School, none
          of us — myself, his teachers, his
          classmates — dreamt that he would amount
          to a hill of beans. But we were wrong.
          And you, Rupert, you were right. And
          that's why tonight, before the entire
          nation, we'd like to apologize to you
          personally and to beg your forgiveness
          for all the things we did to you. And
          we'd like to thank you personally, all of
          us, for the meaning you've given our
          lives. Please accept our warmest wishes,
          Rita and Rupert, for a long and
          successful reign together.
```

The subtext of this scene is, "Rupert Pupkin is a wounded, insecure, arrested adolescent who has delusions of persecution and grandeur." It's the subtext that makes the scene funny.

7. Use symbolism

In addition to subtext, you can deepen the impact of your dialogue by crafting lines that symbolize your characters' traits or journey. Here's an example from *Pulp Fiction*:

```
Butch bellies up to the bar next to Vincent, drinking his
cup of "Plain ol' American."
                         BUTCH
              (to English Dave)
              Can I get a pack'a Red Apples?

                         ENGLISH DAVE
              Filters?

                         BUTCH
              Non.
```

The dialogue symbolizes Butch's character. After this scene, we know he's a straight shooter with no filter.

7. Create a catch phrase for your character

Nothing cements a funny character in the public imagination like a catch phrase. If you've aced the task of making your dialogue unlike anyone else's, there's a good possibility one of your characters will have a signature phrase that could catch on in the popular culture. A catch phrase is the ultimate prize of a funny character. It elevates them to icon status in the minds of the audience, and the character's potential becomes limited only by your imagination.

In the next chapter, let's do some imagining.

11

EXPLOITATION

If you've created a funny character—congratulations! You have an asset. If your character has rabid fans hungry for more stories featuring that character, you have a potentially valuable piece of intellectual property that could pay you money for the rest of your life if you handle it right.

On the other hand, if you haven't produced any work making use of the character(s) you've created, or if you've produced some things but haven't distributed them on any platform, you have an unrealized asset. If this is your situation, get your character in front of audiences. It doesn't matter if it's a novel, podcast, web series, comic book or independent movie. Get it out there. Self-publish it on Amazon and Audible. Upload it to YouTube. Put it anywhere you can. Give fans the opportunity to find it.

If you've already created some entertainment and distributed it to audiences but don't have many fans yet, you probably need to listen to some feedback and tweak your work accordingly. It could probably be improved. Continue to tweak it until you create an entertainment product featuring your character that has the potential to build a fan base.

If you've built a fan base for your character but haven't produced any merchandise or leveraged your character's popularity with any ancillary products, you're poised to exploit your character however you like. You can do one of two things. (1) You can approach a licensing company to see if you can make a good deal with them to exploit your character. (2) You can produce a few items on your own. Make T-shirts, bumper stickers, mugs, or key chains. There are several companies just a Google search away that can make such products. See if your audience will buy them on your website or on a marketplace like Etsy or Amazon. If they do, and if you can turn a profit, you can either keep selling merchandise, or you can reach out to licensing companies again. Now that you have an audience, established products, and a profitable property, you're in a much stronger position to negotiate a good deal for yourself.

If you sell enough on your own, a major licensing company may approach you about buying the rights. Weigh your options carefully. It may be worth your while to sell the rights and collect a small percentage of mechanizing profits if it means you'll be relieved of managing all the manufacturing, accounting, and shipping. Or you may decide it's more profitable to continue selling the merchandise on your own.

If you've already sold your story to a publisher or production company, there's a good chance you also sold your ancillary rights as part of that deal. It was probably in the fine print of the contract. If you haven't signed a deal with any company but think you might, make sure you negotiate those rights before you sign. Retain all of them if you can, but at least get a percentage of gross profits (not net) from any licensing deals and subsequent merchandising sales. There's no standard amount for this. Every deal is different. Some production or publishing companies have no interest in licensing rights, and only buy them because they're part of their boilerplate contract. They might consent to letting you retain 100% of those rights. Others will be keen to exploit any popular characters they invest in, and you may only be able to negotiate a small percentage of merchandising.

If you have such a deal and you've already negotiated a piece of the profits, you'll need to hound the publisher or production company you're in business with and encourage them to make some licensing deals to exploit your character's popularity.

Whatever your situation, you deserve a percentage of the profits of any licensing contracts. It's worth protecting yourself and your potential asset early while you have the greatest leverage. Consult with legal counsel before signing any licensing deals or entertainment-industry contracts.

Regardless of what you do with the funny characters you create with the help of this book, whether you make money on them or not—whether you want to or not—I look forward to seeing them, and having a good laugh at them.

ACKNOWLEDGMENTS

The author gratefully acknowldges the following for their assistance: Dandelion Benson, Tony Bozanich, Paul Case, Max Devin, Tim Grimes, Marcellus Hall, Peter Hilleren, Tim Johnson, Hugh Kelly, Jon Lenaway, Ross Levine, Brian Mallman, Gordon Petry, Jay Rath, Madeline Schmidt, Holly Schwartz, Simon Seline, Jordan Ward, Brooke Washington, Keith Webster, and every member of the gallant street team.

What's the single biggest mistake you make every day writing comedy?

What are the specific lines you're wrting that make your writing awful?

How do you stay on top of the latest pitfalls in the fast-changing world of comedy writing?

Find out in Scott's

FREE EBOOK

Get yours now—along with free comedy tips, tricks and opportuities! Just visit

www.HowToWriteFunny.com/list

Printed in Great Britain
by Amazon